Yes You Do Know One of Us: Stories of Every Day Heroes

RAINN Speaker's Bureau

authorHOUSE®

AuthorHouse™
1663 Liberty Drive, Suite 200
Bloomington, IN 47403
www.authorhouse.com
Phone: 1-800-839-8640

First published by AuthorHouse 4/3/2009

ISBN: 978-1-4389-4201-8 (sc)

Printed in the United States of America
Bloomington, Indiana

This book is printed on acid-free paper.

Forward

"Statistics show that every two minutes someone in America is sexually assaulted. Our society keeps statistics related to assaults reported, but does not include those who did not survive or those who have remained silent. The silence came about because our society has denigrated sexual assault as heinous, which it is. But nowhere do we hear nor read that the victims are not heinous, but are beautiful people who have kept silent out of fear; fear of more attacks on them or their families; fear of being labeled heinous as our society labels the crime; the assault being a license for others to take liberties; affecting the workplace or being threatened in the work place;'(fear that going public with one's story will serve as license for others to take liberties or will result in feeling threatened or discriminated against in one's work environment') There are far too many fears to mention.

The stories in this book are being shared by those who have not only survived, but have the courage to break the silence about what many feel is the unspeakable. They speak their truths even though many of their assailants were not brought to justice. Some victims have not totally healed from their traumas. They stand in their truth because it is time. They stand united in the knowledge they are not alone.

It is the hope of every contributor of this book, indeed, a prayer,that anyone in need of support, love, understanding, compassion, whatever their needs are, will find them in the RAINN Organization, and the RAINN Speaker group. We want the readers to hear our stories and know that we feel their pain and understand those who are silent and why. We also pray the readers understand that as we speak our truth, they will gain insight into the fact that lives can parallel even though traumas may differ.

It's imperative that even if you can't afford help out there, you grab a friend or even a stranger to share your story. Please remember there are many free resources at RAINN including anonymous Internet consulting. Though sharing pain is not easy, we know that the sharing helps to keep the anger from growing stronger within you, as this only creates behavioral disorders. Reaching out for help and speaking out will help to make your spirit free, strong and confident again.

Though people applaud us, our one goal, is your well-being, that you understand above all else that it is time for you, the reader, to stand strong and say, "No more will I be abused; no more will I be silent."

Rev. Lady 'Spirit Moon' Cerelli

www.peacewithptsd.org

Dedication

The authors of this book dedicate their stories to those who can not speak out of fear, shame, lack of courage, or have no voice – the dead tell no tales. We are your friends, family, neighbors, and co-workers. These stories bond us together though we may have never met each other. We do not consider ourselves to be courageous people, but we are tired people. We are tired of any abuse that knows no boundaries in race, creed, religion, age or gender. We speak the unspeakable with voices we pray will stand out as testimony to injustice and social misunderstandings. We speak our truth to give strength to those who feel they have no hope, courage for those with low self-esteem, and compassion for those who no longer *feel*. You see, we have been there and we understand.

As authors of this book, we are all dedicated speakers of RAINN, the Rape, Abuse, & Incest National Network. As Speakers of the RAINN Speakers Bureau, we educate and inform the public about sexual violence and abuse. As members, we all have the opportunity to share our personal stories with students, communities, victim service groups and/or the media. This book is a compilation of many of our experiences as well.

We know that it is difficult to share something so personal, but we believe that sharing our survival story can inspire others who may be victims of sexual assault/abuse to come forward for the first time and receive the help they need. You are not alone and you are strong. We are proud to donate 100% of the profits from this book to RAINN in hopes of educating, preventing, and helping others suffering from abuse and sexual violence.

These stories bond us though we may have never met each other. We do not always consider ourselves courageous people, but we are strong and dedicated people. We are dedicated to preventing others from suffering from abuse and sexual violence. We are dedicated to preventing any type of abuse that knows no boundaries in race, creed, religion, age, or gender.

We speak the unspeakable with strong voices that we pray will stand out as testimony to injustice and social misunderstandings. We speak our truth to give strength to those our voices speak for. You will be heard and you are valued, loved, and deserving of dignity and compassion.

Join us in providing support to those who need it most. Buy this book today and know that you are helping those who have experienced violence and abuse that will forever change their lives and the lives of those around them. Please let them know that they are not alone and they are supported, deserving of justice, dignity, and compassion. Also, become a volunteer for RAINN* giving those affected by sexual violence a safe place to turn when they cannot find their voice. For more info, and to sign up, visit http://www.rainn.org

Contents

A Truly Happy Life
By Michelle McKenzie

I was 14-years-old when a man from my church youth group raped me. This was a catastrophe in my virgin world of purity, godliness and security. My rape wasn't as violent as most. My life wasn't threatened. I had no broken bones, no bruises, no cuts, and no physical pain. I didn't have to go to the hospital. No one knew my trauma from looking at me. I appeared normal to everyone else. However, psychologically speaking, I had been cut to pieces.

I plunged into a downward spiral of self-destruction and hatred. My childhood ended in that instant and I became a recluse, not being able to relate to any of the girls around me. Since my life revolved around the church, all of my friends were also proud virgins. Loosing my virginity was like exiling me to another country. My self-esteem dwindled as I began to believe I was dirty and worthless. I started having horrible nightmares, depression and repeated thoughts of suicide. I spent years not really understanding what happened to me or why I was feeling so miserable.

By the end of high school, I started to understand the significance of that event 3 years prior. I knew I needed to speak to someone about the thoughts that were always racing through my head. I went to therapy for 3 months and then decided to move on with my life. Therapy helped me overcome my suicidal thoughts, learn how to value my life and become excited about starting college. The rape seemed so far away at that point and I wanted to let it go.

After college began, I started to discover myself for the first time in years and let go of the anger that built up throughout high school. Yet, I slowly started being afraid of death, a hidden fear that grew stronger each day. I had horrible thoughts about getting hurt again, and I believed someone was trying to kill me. I was constantly trying to protect myself and never wanted to be alone. These thoughts increased until I had panic attacks five times a week. In addition to panic attacks, I was displaying obsessive/compulsive behaviors, extreme paranoia and anxiety.

I could not see how these issues were related to the rape. I eventually went into therapy for the second time after making a strong determination to live my life without fear. When I finished high school and therapy the first time, I thought my rape issues were over. I was shocked 6 years after the rape to find out how much I was still being influenced by it. It was especially difficult during that time for other people to recognize that I was suffering, because I was so happy when people were around me. I was outgoing, an honors student and in a good relationship. I loved life and wanted to live every moment. Yet, it was with this renewal of loving life that my biggest fears manifested.

At the end of therapy, my fears were gone and I was able to enjoy being alone without constant dread of being hurt. It took me 7 years after the rape to be able to feel safe and even then, it was a process that is continually growing. Feeling safe was the slowest element of my recovery, whether it be driving in my car, sitting in my room or being with someone intimately.

After years of coping from the rape, I came to a point in my life were my spirituality needed healing as well. I left the church shortly after the rape and wanted to connect with a religion that made sense for my life. I started practicing Buddhism shortly after my second round of therapy ended. My conversion to Buddhism allowed me to focus on developing my self-esteem and self-confidence, as well as realizing my mission in life. It was through this process that my healing came full circle. My spirituality was a fundamental part of who I was before the rape, and I never thought that spirituality could be recovered. For me, I wanted to regain everything that had been taken from me by my rapist and this goal was finally achieved.

Healing takes time. The support that we receive from friends and family is invaluable. As I look back at my healing process, I realize that I had to fight in order to overcome my fears, low self-esteem, and many other problems. I had to determine with unwavering conviction that I wanted to be in control of my life and regain all the things that I lost. After I started on the path toward realizing these goals, my healing steadily advanced.

For so many years, I sought out the reason why this horrific suffering had to be a part of my life. As I looked around me, I saw that so many people were suffering, that it is a part of life itself. What really matters is how the suffering impacts our lives. I will no longer allow my rape to take away my happiness. Now, I can say with confidence that I have developed a truly happy life.

This quote reflects my feelings towards being a rape survivor:

> Life is full of unexpected suffering. Even so, as Eleanor Roosevelt said: "If you can live through that you can live through anything. You gain strength, courage and confidence by every experience in which you really stop to look fear in the face. You are able to say to yourself, 'I lived through this horror. I can take the next thing that comes along.'" That's exactly right. Struggling against great difficulty enables us to develop ourselves tremendously. We then call forth and manifest those abilities dormant within us. Difficulty can then be a source of dynamic new growth and positive progress.

Daisaku Ikeda

Sick Day
Anonymous

I am waiting in the counselor's office, hoping he won't come. I keep insisting that I'll be fine; there's no need to call my stepfather.

But I fainted. There's no getting around it. I have to be sent home and he's the one who answered the phone.

He's coming to get me.

They say I'm turning pale again, tell me to put my head between my knees. I do that gladly, hide my face. Hide my fear.

He's here. Very concerned.

"She's just been putting in such long hours lately with that play and everything. She probably caught a bug. I'll run her up to the doctor and get her checked out."

We walk out to the truck. He seems very concerned. The feeling of dread is a rock in my stomach. It causes my body to cave inward on itself, protecting the soft parts, making me small.

We leave the doctor's office with a prescription and instructions for me to rest. It's only 10:00 am. We're alone till 5:15.

He asks if I want something to eat, offers to take me through McDonald's. I decline. He insists on getting me a Sprite and some crackers.

Home now. I go to my room, lie down in my bed, fully dressed, under the covers. Maybe he'll go somewhere. I can sleep. No.

"I canceled my golf game in case you get sick again."

I hear the TV come on.

I close my eyes.

I am startled awake when I hear my bedroom door open. He doesn't turn the light on, but it's still bright in here since it's the middle of the day.

"I brought you some Sprite."

I thank him.

He is walking toward me, reaching for me. I steel myself not to flinch.

He lays his hand on my forehead.

"You still feel warm. I brought you some aspirin. Sit up and take this with some of that Sprite."

I do as I'm told.

He sits on the edge of the bed. The rock is a brick now.

"Is your stomach still upset?"

I say yes, hoping he'll leave it at that.

Wrong answer.

"Let me rub it for you."

He raises my shirt and exposes just my stomach, gently puts his hand on it and starts rubbing in small circles.

"When we were kids, Momma always rubbed our stomachs when we were sick."

I can't move. I've turned to ice.

The circles are getting larger. His hands are coming ever closer to my breasts.

"You're so tense, Vickie. Man, your stomach is tight. You should try to relax."

I can't breathe. I can't stand to look at him.

I turn my head away and stare at the wall.

"I bet these jeans are hurting you. Here, let's get these off of you."

He unbuttons my jeans, unzips them, and pulls them off of me.

Still rubbing my stomach.

Lower.

"Are you aching down here?"

I tell him I'm not.

"Do you think this is a female problem?"

Lower still.

I tell him it's not.

His hand is inside my panties. He is feeling all around.

"Does that hurt? Does that hurt? I can't figure out why you're so sick."

His fingers are inside me. I shut it out. I feel nothing. I do not move.

"Vickie, I think you've got a knot down there. Have you ever noticed that before?"

I tell him no, I haven't.

"You should probably get that checked out. Let me check and see if there are anymore."

He is all over me now. I feel sick. I float away. I feel nothing.

"I don't feel anymore knots. I'll rub this one for awhile, see if it goes away."

"Is that making you feel better?"

I tell him it is not.

"Do you want me to rub harder?"

I tell him I just want to sleep.

"Okay. I'll go away and let you rest. But you call me if you need anything."

Finally, he is gone.

I turn my face to the wall, hoping he doesn't come back.

I think about praying, but don't see the point.

I manage to expand the brick. It is larger, takes me over.

Now my whole body is made of steel. Hard and cold. An impenetrable fortress. Safe.

Finally, I sleep.

Breaking the Chains
© Sara Ylen 2003

My tears started out of fear,
Despair-wondering why?
But never was there answers,
No reason stopped the tears.
I listened-waited-hoped,
Wanting the wind's whisper
To help it all make sense.
But the whispers were too silent
The storms continued brewing.
My head, heart and mind
Shared the same eternal throbbing.
Nothing offered freedom.

Is there freedom to be had?

The chains of fear
Still grip my heart
Fragments of my soul whisper,
"Cut them free!"
But how?
When my tears go unnoticed
And hearts go untouched.
Cries fall on deaf ears
When they should hear the most.
What if each tear
Fell on cheeks not my own and
Carried the sting of my sorrow?
Would the cheeks that they fall on
Pass on inner strength?
Or am I in search of what's already there?

Yes, there is freedom
The day that I find
I've had what I needed-
Possessed the key-
Inside the place that will break out the chains
And melt down the steel in my soul.
To seek what is lost
Means to find what is there.
I'll find that and more with
Infinite searching.
Allowing the sun to break through.
Cobwebs will clear and
What will be left
Will not fear shining through for the world.

He toddles on the kitchen tile
Almost two, I hear him laugh
Tupperware clatters as it hits the ground
Another mess to clean up later

You push me over the kiddy gate
Down the hall to my room
I see your mouth moving
The words make no sense

I smell cheap beer, your eyes are bloodshot
The mirror taunts me and I know
You watched me, wanting
I was not yours then or now

Screaming would scare him, I lay quiet
Almost two, I hear him laugh
He calls "Momma" but I cannot answer
The taste in my mouth is bitter

Every sound in the house fades
My hands cover my face, I see darkness
Paralyzed, there is no fight in me
Tears flow when the front door slams shut

My dress is not torn, just wrinkled
There are no bruises, no marks, no blood
I lay on the floor facing away from the mirror
You can only see me if I let you
By: Candice Amil

Vigil
by Vickie Lamb

I was alone –
The only one who could not sleep when day was done.
I had wounds that would not heal.
I could not laugh. I could not cry. I could not feel.

I hid in silence,
Too ashamed to show my face, to say my name.
Thinking surely there must have been
Something horrible I'd done, some awful sin.

I felt guilty
For the way I walked, dressed, looked, acted, talked.
There was something about me. Every time
They attacked me, I paid for the crime.

I hid my face,
Lost my voice. Many times I made the choice
To stop the pain, the shame, the fear.
I tried to die, but I'm still here.

I fought so hard
to want to live. I found I had something left to give.
My heart, my mind, my very soul.
I gave it all, and I was whole

I invited others
to tell the story that I knew so well.
I heard their grief, their fear, their shame.
I cried their tears, bled their blood, felt their pain.

Millions of victims
At my door, I saw them all, still there were more.

The line stretched farther than I could see.
I learned they were everywhere, just like me.

Every two minutes
Another assault. Another innocent thinks they're at fault.
Too tired to stand, too scared to shout.
A heart breaks down. A light goes out.

Hear me now!
I've made a choice. I speak for those who've lost their voice.
For the broken ones who cannot stand,
I offer an ear, I reach out a hand.

I stand tall,
no guilt, no shame. I show my face. I shout my name.
I hold it high, this candle of mine,
For those still in darkness, I will shine.

"The ax forgets; the tree remembers"
~African Proverb

It was an innocence lost, never to be found again.

My life had been so carefree, so open. One night changed all of that.

The summer of 1999, the year of high school graduation, started off as the best summer of my life. I can't remember a summer that I had been happier. I had the best group of friends in the world and we were all going off to college in a few months. We tried to make every moment with each other memorable. Our days were full of fun and parties. Every weekend was a different graduation or going away celebration.

One party at the end of July steered my world in a whole new direction, though I didn't know it at the time. We were all having a good time talking, laughing and drinking. Some had more to drink than others and I was one of them. A close friend, John*, offered to drive me home. It never crossed my mind to think twice about it. I passed out on the way to my house. When I woke up the next day, all I could remember was John pulling the car over and kissing me. I actually thought it had been a dream. I figured we'd all have a good laugh about my dream at the next party that night. Nighttime came and the party was well on its way. While a group of us were sitting around a fire having a few drinks, I started to tell everyone about my dream. John said he really did kiss me. It wasn't a dream. I was a little surprised and told him I didn't remember the rest of the car ride. "Good," he said. Good? How could that be a good thing? So I kept pushing him to tell me why my memory loss was such a wonderful thing. It took about 20 minutes and two more drinks for him to finally say it. I wasn't prepared for his next words.

John said, "well you passed out, so I whipped it out for you to suck it, but you wouldn't. So I took your hand and had you jerk me off for a bit."

He said it so casually as if it happened everyday. I started crying and yelling at him. People started to stare and my best friends ran over to find out what was going on. After I told the story they were furious. My best friend yelled at him and slapped him so hard the people across the yard could hear the palm of her hand hit his face. Then they took me home.

I decided I was just going to forget about it, because I was so embarrassed. I didn't want anyone else to know about it. I didn't want to be the reason for everyone to hate him. However, one week later the cycle of my world would turn even further.

The night of August 1, 1999 was yet another party to attend. I decided not to drink at this one. I didn't want a repeat of the weekend before. This party was a little boring so a group of us decided to go back to my house since my parents were out of town. We planned to do a little late-night swimming. There were six of us, myself and two of my girlfriends, Brenda* and Darla*, John, his best friend Sam* and Sam's cousin, Mark*. We weren't planning on drinking, but the guys had brought along enough beer for them to have one or two a piece. It wasn't enough for any of them to get drunk though.

While we were in the pool, I stayed as far away from John as I could. He made me nervous. I hadn't realized my nerves shouldn't have been wasted on him.

Darla and Mark started to make out, but the rest of us just ignored them. Brenda and John were at one end of the pool while Sam and I were at the opposite end. I'd known Sam since first grade, so I decided to tell him about the weekend before with John. His reaction startled me. He wasn't shocked, angry or disgusted. In fact, his face was expressionless. He just looked at me and said, "Yeah, I know. He told me all about it." Then he leaned in and kissed me. Now Sam was making me nervous. He leaned in to kiss me again, but I turned my head away. At this point the world seemed to move in slow motion while happening so fast.

Sam managed to get me pinned up against the side of the pool. He kept trying to push his body against mine, but I kept shaking my head as if to say "no" and tried using my hands to push him away. I kept opening my mouth to scream, but nothing came out. Where was my voice? Why couldn't I yell for someone to stop him? I could hear Brenda and John laughing. Why weren't they pulling him off of me?

I wasn't strong enough to fight him off. It felt like hours, I think only minutes had passed. I couldn't understand why no one tried to help me. Shortly after, the guys went home, but the girls spent the night at my house. They kept saying to me, "Wow, I can't believe you had sex with Sam. He's so hot." I didn't know what to say to them, so I just went to sleep. The next day I called one of my friends to bring me to Planned Parenthood to get the "morning after pill." I never told anyone he raped me. I just tried to convince myself I wanted it to happen. I figured I wanted him to do it since I didn't fight hard enough to stop it.

A few weeks went by and I had left for college. I went on with my life not realizing how different I had become.

More than a year later, I finally started to come to terms that there was no way I wanted it to happen. He had raped me. I went to the counseling center we had on campus. I was at a religious university and didn't realize they weren't going to be able to help me. The counselor actually asked me what I had done to provoke it. I didn't know what to say. She told me I should write it down in a journal to "reflect on my actions." I took her advise and wrote it all down, but I never went back to see her again.

When I went home for mid-term break, I gave my journal to my mother to read. She started crying and said she thought something had happened to me, but she was afraid to ask me. She convinced me to go to a psychiatrist. I was afraid to go after my experience with the school counselor, but my mom really thought it was a good idea. I only went to see the doctor twice. The first visit she insisted I had been drinking or doing drugs to go along with it and the second visit was even worse.

She told me, "You seem to have a lot of anger issues toward this boy. You should have him come in so you can confront him about it."

I told her where she could shove her practice and I walked out.

I spent the next two years self-medicating. I drank and smoked a lot of pot. I also took a lot of pills. I would use these things until I blacked out, then I'd wake up the next day and start all over again. Throughout that time, I also had sex with random guys that I had no feelings for and no intentions of forming relationships with. I was on a very self-destructive path.

During the summer of 2002, my mother intervened and suggested I talk to someone from our county's local Rape Crisis center. I didn't want to. I'd talked to people before and they told me it was my fault. Why would this be any different? She talked me into trying it and it was the best decision I ever made.

I ended up learning a lot about myself, what had happened to me and why I was behaving like I was. My counselor, Carol, saved my life. I don't believe I would be here today if it hadn't been for her. I started to change my life and the decisions I was making. I started to open up to people and tell them the truth about everything.

It's been over eight years since that night. There isn't a day that goes by that I don't think about it. Every so often I still run into Sam. Sometimes I panic and start drinking. Most times I just take myself out of the situation and go home. I met and fell in love with a loving man who may not understand all that I have been through, but he listens when I want to talk about it and he holds me when I need to cry over it. I try to take life one day at a time. It may not always work, but I don't give up when it doesn't.

In one night I lost a part of myself I will never get back, but I have promised myself I will never be afraid to tell my story. I never know who it might help.

~Kris Magliarditi

* (Names changed)

All Over Me
© Sara Ylen 2003

Mirror image-
I don't like what I see.
The eyes-windows to the soul.
But I see a mask
Waiting
Hiding
Fear of being revealed.
But what I thought
to be secret
Is all over me.

I feel warm fear spread
Like ants marching relentlessly
As the tingling starts to travel
to my extremities.
Panic settles in them like lead.
I feel the thud as they
Refuse to move.
Fear makes me flush, but
Turns me to ice inside-
Unable to react-
Stuck in one mode.
Wanting to run
But can't take a step--or breathe.
My stomach churns in remembrance
Of the betrayal,
The hurt.

My eyes betray me
As I fight to hide
What lurks deep inside me--
Fear

Betrayal
Mistrust
Guilt.
It's all over me.
Over the way I feel,
The way I shudder
When strangers walk by;
The way my heart pounds
And my stomach knots
When I hear the familiar
Slur in someone's speech--
Intoxicated-
Mesmerizing.
I hear it--
Feel it--
All over me.

My image stares back,
Swollen cheekbones,
Ugly black railroad
Holding it all together;
Keeping the flesh safe
But not hiding the memory.
My fingertips touch my face,
Pulling the memory
As if with a magnet,
And it washes
All over me.

Tears well up
In the windows to my soul,
As the ache settles in
To remind me
How deep the wounds go.
They pierce my body,
Encompass everything,
Betraying all that is

Good
Sweet
Innocent.
These wounds heal slowly
But each glance
In the mirror
Reminds me
That for every one that heals,
There are a thousand more--all over me.

This personal memoir is something I wrote because I hope that it can help someone in need of it. I think that my story can help others who are or have been victims of sexual assault and/or rape. I was a victim of an assault that happened over 2 years ago and after intense therapy, medications and deep soul searching, I am finally able to talk about my experience. I want to reach out to those who are going through the very same thing. I know how helpless and alone it feels to be a victim of rape. I want those to see that there is hope out there. Whether you feel it or not right now…there is. As painful is it may seem, there is a way to pick yourself back up. My goal is to spread awareness and to lend a helping hand to this growing, silent epidemic. This crime occurs more often that we think; unfortunately, it is not spoken about as much as it should. Raising awareness can make both men and women like me feel safer and secure during times of terror and uncertainty. It can shine a light for those who have been in the dark for so long. I thank you for taking the time out to read this. I just hope it can help others who truly need and deserve it. Even if it affects just one soul, that is more than enough for me.
-Julie

Lost Soul

I've come a long way I think. There was a time, not too long ago when I couldn't even write or talk about this without me ending up in tears. Now, more than 2 years later, I am finally ready to tell my story- but as a different person; a stronger person. I am finally ready to share my experience with those who know how lonely it feels, those who have suffered through the constant anxiety and overwhelming sadness, those who have been so traumatized that they can no longer trust anyone around them. Those who have had their souls and self worth ripped from them. Those who feel that it is impossible to love and be loved by any other. I want those to know that they are not alone. The pain they feel is also felt by others and most importantly, I want them to know that there will eventually be a light at the end of this very long, dark and scary tunnel. Only time can tell when and how, but knowing that there is hope can make all the difference. Take it from me, a girl who had absolutely no hope or faith anymore. I thought I was destined to be unloved and alone for the rest of my life. I thought I would never amount to anything. I felt I was the lowest of the low. I felt like no one would ever love me the way I wanted them to. Thankfully, I look back and see that girl as someone else. I was fortunate enough to have the support and guidance I needed to get through this. It definitely took some time to allow myself to accept the help I needed because I am not going to lie; this was not an easy journey. It still isn't. It was a hard, painful and emotionally exhausting time for me. There were moments when I wanted to just give up. Those moments felt like an eternity. Things are finally different now. I have been waiting a long time to feel this way. I see hope. I feel it. I see a bright and better future. Most importantly, I feel better about myself. Things still aren't perfect. I understand that it will take a while for things to fall back into place, but I am definitely in a much better place than before; a lighter place. Rape is not only life changing, it steals. It rips away everything you deem valuable-your self worth, your dignity, your soul. It takes away everything that is vital for living. It takes away who you are. You become numb, dark, and emotionless. That was my biggest struggle…Trying to figure out who I was again.

Don't get me wrong, I was never that happy-go-lucky girl either, before being raped. I think that's what made this whole experience worse for me…I was as self destructive and crazy as they came. This was a result of feeling the repercussions from years of mental and emotional abuse. My father was not the nicest man. In fact, he was selfish, mean and nasty. He was never really loving or supportive. The only thing he was good at was making me feel worthless most of the time. My worst memories of him over powered the few good memories I had of him. I was never going to be good enough, pretty enough, or smart enough in his eyes. It was always "You'll never be like Anna", "If you end up being even half of what Anna is, I'll be happy", or "Look at your Aunt's kids, they are so smart and exceptional. Why can't you be like that?". Anna is my cousin who was (and still is) a brown-nosing, fake bitch. I was surrounded by smart, intelligent kids when I was young so of course I looked like the idiot one when we were all compared. I grew distant. I eventually grew to ignore him, I stopped hearing his words, but I still most certainly felt them. Every insult, every put-down, every cruel comment would feel like a jab to my soul, my heart. The pain was immense, but there was nothing I could do to say or stop it. In his cruel world, he was always right no matter what. Sometimes, his words still taunt me, I still feel the pangs deep within me…I know that his words and actions will always be permanently etched in me. You never forget the things that are said to you from someone who brought you into this world; the good and the bad. Living with him was a nightmare. He didn't treat my mom any better. In fact, he blamed her for me-not living up to his impossible standards. Everything I supposedly did wrong was her fault. It was ridiculous. I still feel guilty to this day because she has done nothing, but support and protect me my entire life. She is my angel who was the complete opposite of him...encouraging, loving and supportive. She showed me loyalty and unconditional love. He broke her heart over and over again. He cheated on her many times; had affairs and relationships with other women. I hated him. I hated that my mom was with him and had to put up with that. I hated that my sister and I had a father like him. I had to get out of there because if I didn't, he would destroy what ever strength I had left.

I was particularly insecure going into college, and so, I drowned all of my anguish and anger in drinking, partying and sex. I was free to do whatever I wanted. I didn't care what I did because I didn't care about myself. At the time, I didn't see it that way, mostly because I was in denial and partly because I did a good job convincing myself that I didn't need anyone. I didn't need relationships or men. I didn't need any of that because I was going to be by myself in the end anyways and that was the way it was going to be. My thoughts about myself were even more detrimental to my well being...I trained myself to believe that I wouldn't need anyone. I was going to end up alone, so I should just get used to it now. In actuality, it was all I ever wanted and needed. Someone. Just someone to love me. It was so sad and pathetic. It was a lonely place, and much like the cliché, I tried to find love in all the wrong places. Aside from that, I chain smoked, and drank too much to ease the pain. I had the best friends anyone could have, but I don't think anyone really saw what was going on inside, at lease I didn't think anyone saw.

Love, or something like it

After college, I became more depressed because I had to move back home with my parents. I was still trying to figure out what I wanted to do with my life. My college plans didn't work out the way I wanted...so I had to start from square one again. My dad was still as cruel as ever, if not worse. I worked constantly to get away...that's when I met Ben. I fell head over heels. He was my outlet. My first love. My first real relationship.

My first everything. To make a long and heartbreaking story short…I loved him, he said he loved me…only to end up leaving after all was said and done. I was devastated. The circumstances behind his leaving left me baffled and confused. I can't even begin to get into it. It was just too unreal to process at the time. I officially went over the edge at that point. I clung onto him for dear life. I relied on him so much and quickly gave him everything and anything I could possible give. His leaving tore me apart. I didn't know what to do. So, I continued to drink, more. I partied. I was promiscuous. I wanted something to fill that void. Of course, those one night stands can only make you feel good for so long and we all know that it only leaves you more empty and alone. My depression got worse, but I didn't care. My obsessive compulsions got worse too. I worked too much, shopped too much, drank too much, partied too much. That ended up getting the best of me. I just wanted the pain to stop. Was that so much to ask? Then Ben came back, throwing more salt on the wound as the saying goes. He should have stayed where we was. He came back and tortured me…I was so heartbroken, so angry, still so in love with him. My worst fear came true – I watched him fall in love with someone else when I still loved him. He ended up leaving again, this time with her only after a month or so. How was that fair? How can someone do that to someone they claimed to have loved, just weeks earlier? That was hard to witness, just when I thought it couldn't get any worse. I put up a nice wall. I pretended I didn't care…I didn't want anyone's pity so I acted like it didn't phase me. In actuality, it was killing me inside.

The Nightmare

My best friend, Serena & I were out one night doing our usual Thursday night routine that consisted of partying, drinking, dancing… just having fun. That was when I met Jake & Tim. I thought Jake was hot. There was something about him. Tim claimed to be the club manager… we later found out that he was a wannabe and was only a club promoter. Anyway, these guys seemed nice enough. Little did I know, I was about to get myself into a lot of trouble. I was lonely and thought, here's a guy who wanted to take me out to dinner. I haven't been out with someone in a while…I needed someone to help me forget Ben. So why not? I thought, Julie, for once, let your guard down a little…that was my rationale. So I agreed to meet him.

I was having a drink with my friend Kelly when Jake showed up to meet me. Kelly left shortly after, so Jake and I proceeded to another bar to talk. I had another glass of wine by halfway through our conversation, I noticed something strange. Jake was acting shady and was not talking much. He even acknowledged that and apologized, claiming that he was tired. Still, I thought it was strange and something didn't feel right. I ignored my instincts and had another glass of wine. By then it had been my 3rd glass, which usually does not do anything for me considering I was such an alcoholic then. I went to the ladies room and when I returned, Jake suggested we go the bar next door to meet his friends. I went along and had Serena meet us there as well...That was the last clear memory I had...Everything else after that moment was a big, cloudy, mess. I didn't remember getting into the bar (which was literally a minute down the road). I vaguely remember seeing Serena there. I didn't remember any of our conversations. Serena later told me that I was wasted beyond belief and thought that I had taken a few shots beforehand, when in truth, I only had 3 glasses of wine. It was all so hazy...I had flashes of the events that took place later that night. I remember being in Jake's truck. Then being parked on the side of the road in the middle of nowhere. I remember Jake mentioning being in the next town over because we were going to Tim's house at that point. We ended up at Tim's house and I passed out.

I woke up a few hours later to both Jake and Tim in the room. I was extremely confused, disillusioned. Was I really here? Is this really happening? Where am I? How did I get here? Why is Tim here? I was so out of it. I knew for a fact that I didn't want Tim there. I had the worst feeling inside of me. My heart started to race. Tim looked at me, then Jake. He said something. I couldn't hear him. I was numb, frozen. I couldn't speak. It was like my body had gone into shock. Before I could fully realize what was going on, it was already happening. Tim was really nasty. He slapped me, really hard. He was saying derogatory things to me...putting me down...he made me feel like such a whore. I finally gathered the courage to tell him to stop. I pushed him off of me. I knew I had to get out of there. I looked at Jake and told him that I wanted to go home. Tim looked at him and told him to "take care of this"...he left the room. I looked at Jake in disbelief. He had been up all night, clearly intoxicated. Granted, I barely knew the guy, but I have never met someone who would ever let something like this happen to a girl HE took out on a date. The asshole had the nerve to tell me that he was sorry and the he wanted to be with me because he had feelings for me. I left the room and ran down the stairs. I started to walk down the driveway. I looked back occasionally, afraid that he would drive after me. He never came out looking for me. At this point, I was trying to keep my composure. I had no idea where I was and how I got there. I tried frantically to call a cab, but I realized that a cab can't pick me up because I had no clue where I was. I remember thinking, Julie, what have you gotten yourself into? How did you let this happen?

Angels sent from above

I looked over to my right and saw an old man walking his dog. I walked over to him and said "Excuse me, sir? I know this is going to sound strange, but can you please tell me where I am?"...I proceeded with a lie due to the incredible amount of shame I felt at the time. I told him that I had just gotten into a fight with my boyfriend and I just left his friend's house, I told him that I needed to know where I was so that my friend could pick me up. The old man, with so much concern on his face asked me if I was OK and if I felt that I was in any trouble. I said no, I just wanted to go home. He offered to drive me to a more well known location so that my friend can find me. I agreed. He walked back to his house and a few minutes later, drove back down with his precious wife in the car. They were so kind. So gracious. They took me back to reality-back to safety and comfort. They dropped me off at a gas station where Kelly picked me up. Right before I got out of the car, the man's wife said to me "Well, I hope you end things with this boyfriend of yours because he most certainly didn't leave you in such a safe situation." I just nodded. Little did she know. Kelly was my savior that day. Ironically, she was the friend who left me with Jake. So much can happen in just 12 hours. As soon as I got into the car, I broke down. I was in absolute shock and disbelief. Is this really happening? I couldn't even bring myself to relay the details of what happened to Kelly. She got the short hand version and offered to take me to the hospital. I refused. I wanted to go home. I wanted to sleep...forever, if possible. I just wanted to forget

Reality Sets In

Shortly after Kelly dropped me off at home, I ran into the bathroom and threw up. I threw up all morning. I didn't know what was wrong with me. I felt so sick. I felt disgusting. I immediately showered to get all the nastiness off of me. I still smelled him. He reeked of stale cigarettes. I felt his presence looming over me. I still heard him. I finally fell asleep. I awoke to what seemed like a million missed calls and voice mails. There were even calls from Jake. The nerve of that guy! From then on, Jake would continue to call me, leaving me messages as if nothing had happened. He even tried asking me out again. Every single one of his calls went unanswered. As if that day couldn't be any worse…Among the other missed calls was a message from my friend MacKensie. Her boyfriend, a friend of mine, had passed away that morning. My emotions were on overload. I felt like I was going to explode. Kelly stopped by later that day. She saw the bruises on my legs and thighs. She was in shock too. It finally sunk in…something really horrible just happened to me. The question that constantly plagued me was, "is this rape?"…it was such a gray area. We all know about the typical scenarios when rape occurs. But what about my situation? In this instant, I wasn't sure. For the continuing months after, that question would constantly haunt me. *Yes it was rape, because you were intoxicated. No it wasn't-you put yourself in this situation. Yes it was-you never wanted to have sex. He forced it on you because you were incapable of saying no. You never said yes. NO-you let this happen! YES-he should never have been in that room in the first place. NO it wasn't-This is all your fault!* Either way, I was drenched in shame and humiliation because I thought it was my fault. All I knew was that I was never going to be the same. I saw my GYN and told her what had happened. The physical exam confirmed that an assault took place. I refused a rape kit. I refused to report it to the police. I just wanted to forget and move on. In retrospect, I had no idea what was to come.

I don't even remember how I broke the news to Serena, but she immediately came to my rescue. She continued to be there for me, protecting me, sticking up for me, speaking out for me when I couldn't do it myself. She was the first person who made me disclose the horrifying details of that night. It was the hardest thing to do. I could barely gather the courage. It was difficult hearing the words. I still remember that day…we were sitting outside of Starbucks, smoking our cigarettes. She sat and listened as I tried to recall the events. That was when we began putting the pieces together. After only 3 glasses of wine, I was inebriated beyond belief. I blacked out. I was so sick the next morning. That was when we figured out that I must have been drugged. My behavior that night and the events there after just didn't make any sense. There were so many other times when I would drink in excess but was still able to recall the events of the night. That night though, I knew I wasn't in the right state of mind to consent to sex. My instincts were telling me the same thing. Regrettably, by then I couldn't prove anything anymore. I just wanted to forget it all. I wanted to move on. Unfortunately, that wasn't so easy. Months of anxiety and depression followed. Serena felt guilty for leaving me that night. It wasn't her fault. After that, we were extra careful whenever we were out. She made sure I was never alone. She made sure never to leave my side. I actually remained sober for awhile…that didn't last long. Once again, I drowned myself in work. I cried every night. I drank alone or whenever we went out. I drank to the point of hysterics. Crying, feeling so horrible about myself. I felt so alone.

This occurred over a course of 6-9 months. Believe it or not, I even ran into Tim a few times after that. Every single time, I froze; unable to speak. I felt like he took something away from me…dangling it in my face. Taunting me. For awhile, he still had that control. That smirk he had on his face…I have never hated someone so much. By then I had opened up to a few more friends and some even got into a confrontation with him. I didn't have the courage to speak up for myself; Serena had to do it for me. My friend Luke almost killed him one night. I wanted everything to go away. I wanted him to stay away from me. I didn't care if he fell off the face of the earth. He was scum. The last time I saw him was when Serena confronted him and told him to stay away from him. This was after a few failed attempts to talk to me. I could not believe the nerve of this guy. "Don't look at her, talk to her, or even stare at her direction", Serena told him. "You know what you did.".…He responded with, "OK…OK, I'm sorry." That response validated everything I was afraid to believe. That I was indeed raped…most likely drugged…and I *knew* he knew. I felt it, my gut knew it. His acknowledgment relieved me in a way, because for the longest time, I felt like it was my fault; that I was the crazy one. From then on, I always stayed away from the guys. I was reluctant to give anyone any part of me. I always kept my distance. I always found an excuse to turn them down. I grew angrier…at times, as ridiculous as it sounds, I would blame Ben. If he hadn't left, I wouldn't be here. I now know that he wasn't good for me either. There was a reason why he left. It would take me almost 3 years to figure that one out.

Pushing through the Pain

The pain and the horrible thoughts that I constantly had were killing me inside. I barely talked about it. I didn't tell a lot of people, terrified of their judgments. I was still so ashamed, so afraid of what they would think about me. To this day my own family doesn't even know, and I intend on keeping it that way for now. They wouldn't understand. Maybe one day, I can gather the strength. Instead, I do have my "other" family...my friends, who were and still are so great to me. Loving me unconditionally was what helped me, but I knew it wasn't enough. My destructive behavior led me to a few close calls while drinking and driving. I vowed never to drink and drive again. That was my cue to do something before my life spun completely out of control. No one knew that. Through the helping hands of a good friend, I met Jane, my therapist. She had such a calming nature to her. She made me feel safe and good about myself. Most importantly, she reminded me that it was not my fault. I've been with Jane over a year now and I have made significant progress. I felt better talking about things with her especially when I felt I couldn't go to anyone else. I needed it. We worked for a few months without any medications because I was hesitant about doing that for many reasons. Almost a year went by and though I felt better...I was still hysterical at times...still anxious. Jane was always very respectful of my decision not to go on meds, but this time I knew I needed to. My chronic depression had lapsed into a physical ailment by then. Plus, I was just so tired. So exhausted from feeling so bad and so low. I could no longer walk with my head held high. I could no longer look anyone in the eye. I was consumed with shame and feeling worthless. I was tired of that. That year I suffered my first few panic and anxiety attacks. There was one night in particular...I felt like I couldn't breathe. I felt like I was going to die. I was restless. I couldn't sleep. I finally saw my doctor and he started me on Effexor. It has helped me tremendously. Maybe one day, I won't need the meds anymore, but it has definitely been a relief. I felt a huge weight lifted.

Finding myself again

Since then, I have managed to quit smoking and the binge drinking. I finished school and passed my national board exam for Cardiac

Ultrasound. I have a terrific job. I have managed to work through the anxiety and the trauma. I slowly opened up to other friends about my situation. And I am not going to lie; I still have my bad days. It is hard to find that balance, but I have come to accept that this is going to be a life-long process. I have realized that I can only take life one day at a time. I am in a different place now; a happier place. I don't even remember the last time I truly felt this way. I have found my light. My job as a Cardiac Technologist brings me the best feeling in the world. I love my career and I have never felt more accomplished. I love my friends more than ever and most importantly, I began to love myself. More than I ever did. I was the one who brought myself here after everything that I have been through. I overcame the trials and tribulations that I have encountered. I pushed and fought through the pain, the sadness…that dark place that I have inhabited for so long. I have stopped being that self destructive, careless girl and I became that strong, courageous woman that I have always wanted to be. I have grown up tremendously…I have amazing people in my life who are willing to do anything for me and I will forever be grateful for that. The mere awareness of all good things in life makes living so much more valuable. Like I said before, the days aren't always sunny and perfect. There are still times when I feel myself slipping a little…still aching…still insecure. But I think it will always be that way. There is something bittersweet about this breaking point. You're saddened by the things that have occurred, but at the same time you are so lucky because it made you fight…it made you stronger.

Fortunately, I am lucky to be with a man who is patient with me… who cares about me, and most importantly, someone who has proven to me that they are not all the same. I am able to feel the intensity of love again…the passion…I am able to simply care. I can finally trust again. And now that I am able to focus on my own needs, I have decided to reach out and help others focus on theirs as well. This is something I have always known I wanted to do, because every rape victim deserves that chance. I am finally ready to speak out. My heart breaks every time I hear or read a story about a rape case. I cringe when jokes are made. I feel for that girl whose life is changed in that instant. Though there are many other cases out there different from my own, it all comes down to the same loss. We all had something taken away from us that moment. Something that will take a long time to get back…the key thing to

28

remember is that you will get it back…One Day. You can not let him win. Whatever it takes, you will find that strength to overcome this and become something I am proud to call myself…a survivor. I finally feel free…I finally have my life back. I am *living* again. I came out on top, better than ever…stronger than ever…and that is something he can never, ever take away again.

Just know that you are not alone…there are people out there willing to listen and help. You'll find your light eventually. Be patient, stay strong. You will survive too. Take it from me.

The day my daughter was born my first fear was how I would protect her from her grandfather, my father, who had molested me as a child.

When it began is a bit fuzzy but it continued for years until one day he warned me we would have to take precautions so I wouldn't get pregnant. I finally told him NO and that I would tell mom. He backed away, reluctantly.

As I blossomed into a teenager I had a boyfriend all through high school but never would go all the way.. Was it the fear of him finding out I wasn't a virgin? I remember I kept a diary and my sister broke into my locked box to show the diary to my mother. I came home to find my dad alone to deal with me and I was more worried that he would try to molest me again then the ramifications of what was contained in the diary.

I went away to college and had a few boyfriends, the first of whom I told I had been molested and he immediately broke up with me. I never told my first husband. Our marriage only lasted 4 years. Perhaps it was the secret I was keeping from him. After having my daughter with my second husband I could no longer keep the secret. Actually we were in marriage counseling with a counselor for veterans (my husband is a Vietnam Vet) and she point blank asked me if I had been abused as a child. I finally confided in someone. But the agony just began. I immediately distanced myself from my mother, father and family and my only means of support was my husband. I became a manic depressive and to this day remember the agony of not being able to get out of bed for days. I lost 75 lbs. and drifted through days. Counseling came to the point where I had to confront my father and finally my mother. I was more afraid of confronting my mother as I feared she would not believe me. The confrontation with my father went better than I would have expected. He told me he was sorry and begged for my forgiveness. Next I had to tell my mother. She was as supportive and agreed to counseling. Eventually our family mended only to find out a few months later my father had cancer and died. However, I am glad I was able to confront my father before his death and to hear him ask my forgiveness was very healing. And my husband and I no longer have any secrets between us.
Diana Dunham

The Water Is My Sky
By Karen Strandskov

I strongly believe that every thing that has happened in my life, mostly good and a little bad, has happened for a reason. There are no coincidences in my life. I might not know the reason for something happening until years later or it may be discovered in the next minute. There is a positive that can come out of any situation. I grew up in the 1950's and 1960's in a suburb a half hour west of New York City. When I was three I started taking tap dance lessons. From that day on I was always involved in physical activities, which proved a benefit to me throughout my life. I believe sports gave me the ability to focus and to be competitive. Sports are also partly responsible for my strong will. I grew up in a home where there were no racial slurs. I never heard my father say the word hate. I feel very strongly that I need to talk about my life from ages eleven to sixteen. The events that occurred during these years explain my intense and immediate reactions to the traumatic event of being raped and sodomized and the aftermath of a criminal trial—before, during, and after. Those years of living with my mother are important because they started off a chain of events that I would turn into positives in order to go on with my life.

My mother was a great mother until she slowly started to show signs of psychosis and this illness was fed by her taking large amounts of prescribed barbiturates—seconal, milltown, and so on. This I will never understand, except for the fact that the psychiatrist was paid very well. He would open his store to give my mother these pills. I would see my mother give him money. I saw extreme husband abuse, as my father was the target of her rage. My father never raised a hand to her and he never said a negative word about my mother to me or my brothers.

At age fourteen, I began living alone with my mother. Both my brothers went to prep school and my father left thinking she would calm down since he was the target of her rage. During this time, I became the target of her abuse. Her drug use had brought her to the point where she was incoherent all her waking hours. My mother lived a life equal to an alcoholic except there were no sober periods. The only food she consumed was what I spoon fed her as she laid on the couch. Daily, she would remind me what she thought of me—I was a murderer like my father and I was a terrible person. I was so happy when our maid Mabel came up for the night, as I was finally able to leave my mother's side and sleep in my own bed. Most nights, though, I would carry or drag her up the stairs at night when she felt like going to bed and sleep where my father had slept. I had to sleep next to this woman, who on some nights, right before bed would try to choke me. As I worked to pry her hands from my throat I would scream at her, staring into her marble-like eyes, until she snapped out of her trance and realized who I was. If I looked at her the wrong way she would sit on the floor and bang her head against the wall until she made a hole. Later, she would hang a picture over the hole which was two feet from the floor. There were a few pictures at this height around the house. I lived out of a suitcase a lot of the time, moving from place to place, because she did not want my father to know where she was, thinking he could "kill her". One summer my mother, I, and two dogs, stayed at a Holiday Inn. She would order room service and every night would flip the tray onto the floor. I would pick up the food and eat what I could. I saw my father once during these two years, when I swam on the winning freestyle relay for the A.A.U. New Jersey Junior Olympics. I couldn't wait to go to school and swim practice where I could be around coherent people. I had developed a sense of humor as a survival mechanism. I still possess my sense of humor—one of the positives that came from the situation. In the long run, I forgave my mother, for I would not have wanted to live her tortured life. Ultimately, my time with her ended when a police chief who was the uncle of a friend of mine saw my mother and said I could not stay with her. I was told if I did not have a place to go I would have to go to a school for girls in Newark. Fortunately, I had my father who was more than anxious to have me live with him. I had stayed with her as long as I did because I thought she would die if there was no one there to physically care for her. I endured much more at the hands of my mother, however I feel the above is adequate to understand the way I handled my rape. I do believe in brain washing. After hearing my mother say numerous times a day over two years that my father was a killer and a very bad person I started to think that maybe that was a possibility. I was fourteen to sixteen during this time. I feel bad, looking back forty years later, that I had those thoughts.

I flunked out of college in my junior year because the abuse was catching up with me. Emotionally I shut down and the anxiety would close my throat when I tried to talk. I started seeing a psychiatrist. I also have a chemical imbalance where my brain receives one tenth of the seritonin that is received by a 'normal brain'. I was told by him that this imbalance would not be as extreme as it was if I had not gone through the abuse with my mother. I was put on anti-anxiety and anti-depressant medication. These medications lessened the anxiety, but did not erase it. Through hard work in therapy the anxiety was reduced. I feel frustration that some of my family members compare me to my mother because I take "pills". The pills my mother took made her unable to function. The pills I take allow me to function and without them I will slur my words because of the height of anxiety. I do not know what is so hard to understand. I had shut down emotionally. Because of being the only girl, I associated all my emotions and behavior with those of my mother. I remember vividly the psychiatrist telling me my mother did not have a patent on emotions. During this time I always saw a light at the end of the tunnel. I knew I could retrieve my personality, and the good times—the times before I lived alone with my mother—would return with all the laughs. After working with the psychiatrist for five years I was able to return to a job where I had to converse with people. I was hired by 7-11 in West Caldwell, N.J. On New Years Eve,(1976-1977), I worked with a co-worker for the first time. When we went in the back storage room to count the money I was caught off guard as this man proceeded to rape and sodomize me. I still have a blank out as to how he got me from the front of the storage room to the back where I remember him trying to get my jeans off. I was resisting him until he slapped the side of my head. My ear was bruised. I went into a survival mode by partially shutting down the feelings of my body from the waist down. When I got back on my feet after the rape I grabbed a bottle from a shelf and smashed it on the floor. I was in a blind rage. If he had not let me out of the store I can not say what I would have done to him. I went to the police who took me to the hospital. There, the nurse performed a rape exam. They said I was slurring my words. After talking to my psychiatrist they learned that my high anxiety was the reason for my slurred speech. In the following weeks I called the area supervisor of

7-11 regarding workmen's compensation. My supervisor informed me that I "was not hurt 'physically!'" Seven Eleven had been grossly negligent because they did not follow the hiring procedures when hiring the man who raped me. He was a smooth talker and thus got hired without the mandatory background check. If the background check had been run on him it would have come back showing he was out on bail for an alleged rape with a knife to the woman's throat. He had the keys to the store the night that he raped me. Seven Eleven paid me a whopping $11,000 for their extremely gross negligence. During the four and a half months between the rape and the trial I took a course at Essex County Community College to keep my mind busy and played a lot of racquetball. I forgave the man who raped me for my own well being. I did not want any negative feelings inside of me. The forgiveness did not mean I would not fight tooth and nail to get him convicted. I knew I could get justice with peace in my heart. During this four and a half month period I lost forty pounds. I felt the less of me that existed, the better. After he was convicted I started eating again. The jury was out twenty minutes, returning a guilty verdict of rape, sodomy, and lewd and lascivious acts. If I had not pressed charges I could not have lived with myself. I was on the stand for approximately six hours. Being on the stand was not a traumatic situation. In fact, I was looking forward to confronting my rapist in an atmosphere where he could not harm me. At one point the defense attorney put my underwear in front of me. I knew he wanted me to say my underwear was called "bikini underwear". When he first shouted at me as to what kind of underwear they where I said "one size fits all". The second time, raising his voice higher asking me the same question, I looked inside the underwear and said "Sears". I knew exactly what he wanted me to say and I was not going to give him the satisfaction. This was not relevant. When I said "Sears" I heard the judge trying to control his laughter as he turned his head to the right away from me.. Some of the jury let out a laugh. The defense did not ask me anymore questions about my underwear. When the man who raped me stared at me, I stared back until he put his head down. The man who raped me took the stand. At this point I could sit in on the testimony as the prosecutor had decided not to call me on rebuttal. He just dug himself deeper into a hole. He was so stupid and his testimony was very pathetic.

He was giving specific times that things happened like "11.43 p.m." By sitting in the courtroom I could tell the prosecutor what things that he said were lies. There were no clocks in the back room and he did not have a watch on. I never cried over the rape. Instead I got mad that this man had the nerve to put his hands on me without my consent. I believe I got angry due to my involvement in sports and my competitiveness. . The night of the verdict my father's lawyer called and asked me if I wanted the rapist killed. He said he knew guards in prison and accidents happen. I said no. I knew he was probably being raped in prison. But that was a result of his choice—because he chose to rape and sodomize me. My college roommate believed I was handling the rape so well because of what I had gone through with my mother. I was told by my therapist this reaction to rape was common among women who were emotionally and physically abused in their childhood. The rape did not destroy me because I had endured my past. I do not know how long the rape took, but my mother's abuse went on daily for years. To this day nothing can be as bad as living alone with my mother. I can not change what happened in my teens. Thus, I have put the experience into a positive, for I am able to handle anything that life might throw at me. I had a lot of support from male figures in my life. My father was my pillar of strength. He was my role model. He taught me how to forgive. My brothers were there for me as well as my male friends, especially Jim C. With this male support, I was able to avoid believing all men were rapists. The man who raped me represented himself only. I would never let the anxiety win. When I went two steps back I would push to go five steps forward.

I went to the trial of this man's other victim. I sat down in the front row right behind the defense table. The defense attorney had me called into the judge's chambers because I was making the guy who raped me nervous!!. He was also concerned that I would make an outcry because the jury could not know that he was in prison for raping me. I went right back into the courtroom and plopped myself right behind him. I wanted him to feel me breathing down his neck. I wanted "me" to be "his" worse nightmare, not vice versa.

I was given workmen's compensation once the man who raped me was convicted. However, five months after my trial I was asked to work at a racquetball club as the Woman's Pro and social director. I had very high anxiety about working and contemplated staying on worker's compensation. Between the rape and the trial, I had played endless racquetball, so I had honed my skill. Racquetball had also been great therapy, being able to hear the crack of the ball against the wall. I will never regret going off worker's compensation. I met so many nice people during the amateur circuit. My dear friend to this day Flo, listened to me when I would talk about the rape. I never felt embarrassed or felt like the rape was my fault. Flo, was a godsend. She would have me laughing so hard my stomach would hurt. I could not wait to go to work. On a daily basis I laughed so hard I couldn't breathe. I played four years on the amateur circuit. When I moved from N.J. in 1981 I was ranked first in the county where I lived. My doubles partner, Pam Palumbo, and I were ranked first in the state of N.J. in Woman's Doubles. I also had attained the ranking of second in the country in Women's thirty and over. Racquetball did so much for my self-esteem. In five years I had gone from not being able to express my voice or my personality to being the social director at a racquetball club. At this time, I have my own tax preparation business. Most of my clients are people I knew from the racquetball club. Sports pulled through once again!

This past Christmas, my best friend from high school told me I was the strongest person she had ever met. That meant a lot to me. Thank you, Lynda. As I said above, things happen for a reason. My experience with my mother made it easier to handle the rape. The rape gave me my voice back as I testified on the stand. I believe all the moments in my life, from the day I was born, have contributed and played a part in who I am today. I love my life today and to me that is all that matters. I believe something like this:

"There's bound to be rough waters and I know I'll take some falls

With my Dad as my captain I can make it through them all."

Garth Brooks

I dedicate my story to my father, Frede B. Strandskov. From the day I was born, I observed his unconditional love, kindness, and respect towards others, especially toward my brothers and myself. He forgave my mother saying "She gave me three beautiful children". I do not know what I would have done during my life without him. He was both a mother and father to me. He was not big on words, but his actions spoke volumes. He was the true meaning of the word gentleman, for he was a gentle man. He was best known for his sense of humor. To my best friend, you are still with me, guiding me. I LOVE YOU and THANK YOU FOR BEING MY DAD.

Dreams
Kate Riffey

When I heard people talk about date rape or young girls getting raped I thought that they had been doing something unsafe that led to that end. I knew it wasn't their fault and the guy had no right to rape them, but at the same time there was something they could have done. In all the orientation classes and advice I got from people my freshmen year of college agreed with that reasoning. Don't drink with people you don't trust, always guard your drink, don't wear suggestive clothing, don't walk home alone at night, don't talk to strangers online and agree to meet them alone… we've all heard it. Sometimes I almost wish I had been doing one of those things when it happened to me, because then it would be something that I could have controlled. Then I could say "well I shouldn't have done that" or pass on some words of wisdom to the next potential victims. As it is, I have no tips or tricks to pass on to keep you from getting raped, abused or attacked, but I do have something to pass on to you after it happens. And if it never happens to you it will happen to someone you know, probably several someones, because that is how prevalent rape is.

My first semester freshman year of college was pretty rough as far as freshman years go. I left my family behind in beautiful Austin, TX and moved to downtown Atlanta, GA to attend college at one of the best and hardest engineering schools in the U.S. I was confident, optimistic, excited, the usual, but halfway through the semester severe depression hit. I literally slept for a month. I finally went to a therapist on campus and was diagnosed with depression and anxiety disorder. I was prescribed Lexapro and twice monthly therapy sessions. Slowly, things improved. The therapy left me feeling more depressed afterwards due to a bad student therapist, but the Lexapro, support from home and the conviction to fight this new found hurdle drove me onward and upward. (Beware the bad therapist) When I went home for Christmas break I had applied to move out of the dorms into an actual house on campus in hopes of improving my situation. I went back feeling resolved that this was going to be better and I had a handle on things.

A week after I had moved into the house I woke up that Friday morning feeling physically numb, I had several small bruises on the inside of my thighs, I was dizzy, but most importantly I remembered a dream I had just had. There was a guy and he was raping me. It was disgusting, pathetic and left me scared. I sat there for a few minutes trying to figure out what had happened, if anything, and then what to do about it. Finally, I called a friend back home. An older woman who had mentored me in high school and who I knew had been raped as well. I asked her what to do, if there was some way to know. Finally we agreed that going to the hospital and getting a rape kit done was the only way to figure out what was going on. Friday evening a friend from home that had also come to Tech, and I entered the hospital at 6pm. We didn't leave until 5:30 the following morning. I spent almost 12 hours in one of the worst hospitals in Atlanta. Unfortunately I was told that it was the only hospital in town that did rape kits. They gave me a room and I proceeded to wait 8 hours. During that time an assigned counselor came and went. She was supposed to guide me through this ordeal, instead she stayed long enough to introduce herself and ask if I wanted a coke. She left to go gossip with the nurse's station outside. I never did get that coke. Around 3am the doctor finally came in and proceeded with the kit. The kit consists of stuff I'm not willing to write about, I'm sure you can Google it, but let me tell you it hurts. A lot. Especially when you have a nurse that had never done one before and a doctor who could care less. Afterwards they gave me shots and pills that are supposed to protect against any STDs and pregnancy. They never did give me any answers as to what happened. Even through I repeatedly asked for a drug test, to see if I had been drugged, I never got one. I asked to file a report, but I never talked to a police officer. Two hours later we were finally allowed to leave. I pretty much slept all the following day.

I woke up late afternoon and decided I wasn't going to let this get me down, it was probably just a bad dream anyway. I went out, got some food, rented some movies and went back to the house. There was a party going on. I went to the fridge for a glass of water and a guy from next door leaned over me to get something. At the time I didn't think anything of it. I took the water and my stuff up stairs and closed my door. At first taste the water tasted weird. It tasted like Tylenol without the coating. I locked my room door and tried to decide what to do. I remembered something my brother had given me over Christmas. It was half in jest, half serious and I'm curious as to what had prompted him to give them to me. It was a package of date rape drug test strips he had found in a store. You put a drop of your drink inside the white ring on this strip and if it turns blue then your drink has been drugged. I'm sure you can see where this is going; the water from my cup did indeed turn the strip blue. I tried it twice, same reaction and then I tried it with tap water, no reaction. In the process of going through these actions I couldn't help notice that someone tried my door handle, finding it was locked they left me alone, for now. Someone just lost on the way the bathroom right? I called my friend again and we took the water and the test strips to the campus police and proceeded to tell them everything that had been going on. They were at a loss as to what to do about it. I spent the night with my friend and in the morning we went down to the Atlanta police station.

I filled out a report and left the strips with them, the water we were told to take to another hospital and see if they could test the contents. The detective then told me that even if they could figure out what drug was used and even if they rape kit came back positive there was nothing they could do about it. They would have to send everything to their lab which was backed up over a year and even if they did get results back they had women come in who knew their attacker(s) and they still couldn't do anything about it. Never the less we took the water to the hospital and waited for four hours before a doctor came and told us they didn't do that kind of testing and we'd have to hire a private lab to do it. It was at that moment that I finally came to realize and accept that there was no one in that town that could tell me what the hell happened to me and there was no one that was willing to help. I sank to the floor in the middle of the hospital and bounced back and forth from crying to panic attacks for awhile. It was Sunday evening and I finally called my parents and told them what was happening. It wasn't that I had been afraid to tell my parents earlier it's just that I didn't want to alarm them if it turned out to be all just a dream. Besides, you try telling your mom who loves you very much and whose 900 miles away that something as awful and traumatic as rape has happened. I was hoping someone would be able to tell me what had happened and the thought of never finding out left me feeling helpless. By Monday morning my dad was there and I decided to pull out of school for that semester. I couldn't imagine going to classes every day like everything was fine. And I of course couldn't go back to the house or the dorms for that matter. I had my car with me so we drove back to Austin.

I don't remember much from the drive, for a while everything was just a haze. I know we took our time and stopped to look at a famous battle field somewhere. We stopped in Louisiana and spent the night with my grandparents who had been briefed on what was going on. They didn't press me for anything, my grandma left me with a book from one of her favorite series. (The Cat Who...) I don't really remember anything from then till about 3 months later when the fog slowly started to lift. During that time I know I got a job working for an awesome lady, I know I found a good therapist and finally started my progress on the depression and occasionally we talked about the rape. I know that I went out and collected every Cat Who... book written to date and read them all. I love cats and the books were a very welcome distraction from reality. Slowly things started to settle down. I received a lot of support from close friends, relatives and mentors. Talking about it and telling people the truth of why I was home suddenly was never really a problem. My brother had more of a problem talking about it than I did. The things that pissed me off the most were the noisy parents of academically competitive "friends" from high school that thought I had come home because I failed out or couldn't handle it. I wanted to scream at them and have them look me in the eye when I told them the truth. Not that it would have really changed their contempt, but I at least would have been able to justify myself. Nights were the worst. During the day I had work, therapy, people around. At night when the lights dimmed and the house went to sleep I'd sit staring at the walls of my room looking at a lot of the same stuff that was in my room in Atlanta. In an effort to relieve the depression and sleeplessness I'd alternate between chapters in a book, petting one of the three cats in the house and drinking.

For the longest time I had the intent to return to Atlanta when everything was settled down. I had worked hard to get in to that school and I didn't want to just give up. My therapist was very against me going back, she said to pick anywhere, but there. At the time I didn't think it would be that bad for me, but I know now that going back would have been a horrible mistake. I searched the internet for colleges with interesting summer programs. Much to my mom's dismay I stumbled upon the University of Alaska. I had always wanted to go to Alaska and here was a chance to go for the summer and have some fun. Mom was furious. Look what happened the first time I moved away and that was only 900 miles away, now I wanted to go to Alaska?! "If something happens" she said, "we won't be able to come get you." Somewhere though, underneath the fog, the fear and anxiety, the self-doubt, somewhere in my core there was a deep and unwavering feeling that this was exactly what I needed. I assembled all the information on the school I could find, all the information about the surrounding area, listed reasons why I should go, why I would be fine, and handed them to my mom in a neat little packet. When I started saving for the plane ticket she realized I was dead serious. My therapist was all for it, it would get me outdoors and be a nice break away from everything to figure out what I wanted to do with myself.

I'll never forget my first two weeks up in Alaska. I was so excited, dead scared, but so very much excited. The first week I threw myself into student activities, checked out all the summer things you could do and made lists of where I wanted to go and how to get there. I noticed how friendly everyone was. Maybe it was the relaxed, open attitudes that Alaskans naturally have or maybe I just started appreciating people being nice. A hug from a fellow traveler, a "good luck with courses", a free piece of pie, everywhere I went and everyone I met seemed to confirm that this was the right decision. Two weeks after I had moved up I joined a school-sponsored trip to go on a 5 day hiking trip through the Brooks Range. The Brooks Range is part of the Arctic National Wildlife Refuge and is about 2-3 hours into the Arctic Circle. I borrowed money from my parents to get the gear I needed, ignored the likelihood of not being physically ready for something like this and jumped into it. Physically I was not ready for it, but mentally I soared. It was beautiful, it was tough, it was challenging, it involved bloody feet from blisters, cold nights, and tough hiking, but afterwards I had never felt so proud. I had never felt so empowered. Being surrounded by mountains, so many wild animals that I had never seen before put me in touch with nature as well as my self.

By the end of the summer I felt I had my self-confidence back. By no means was I over the rape, I knew it was going to be a long haul, but I was happy. I was independent; I had learned so much about my true strength. I had climbed mountains figuratively and physically, and it was AWESOME! By the end my parents had loaned me a total of $4000 to fund something they were very much against and I don't think they will ever know how much that meant to me. To know that even though they didn't agree with my decision, even though they were so scared to let me go, they still helped me financially and through moral support. The month of January was the month that my life got turned upside down, that summer my life got turned around and pointed in a new direction. One I was much happier about.

8 months after I was raped I got an email from a friend back in Atlanta. The message was simple: "What happened to you, happened to me. I need to talk." I immediately called her up and we slowly worked through the process of what to do, whom to tell, where to go. It was long and painful and it brought a lot of memories back to me. However, it opened up an interesting door. There were many others, thousands all over this country that this has happened, is happening, or will happen to and they will need help. Slowly, I started telling my story, first online, where I didn't have to look at anyone or watch their reaction. Then in a few of my classes as presentations, then I started organizing sexual abuse awareness programs on my campus. I'm not going to say this was comfortable to me, that I just flowed into this. My stomach still cramps up and I get nervous when I'm telling my story to a group of people, but then afterwards I hear someone say how much it made a difference to them. How it made them feel like they could tell their story and finally be heard after years of silence and fear.

A year after the rape I finally let go. I stopped telling myself that anytime now I would move back to Atlanta and stick my nose to the grindstone. I realized that my life did not need to go in that direction, and I don't even think it was supposed to go in that direction. I settled down permanently at the University of Alaska, I'm majoring in Environmental Science and I hope to help stop global warming. I'm still sharing my story with others; I still get scared when a stranger gets too close. Sometimes I still get depressed at night when no one else is around, I still have a few nightmares every now and then, and even though I'm very happy with the way things are going I still have doubt. But then I remember the journey I've made and I look around at the surrounding mountains, the random eagle or moose and I feel at peace, I know for sure that this is where I'm supposed to be right now.

A year and half after the rape my whole family came up to Alaska to visit me. They were only able to stay a week, but they got to see the University, the Arctic Circle, Denali, Fairbanks and they loved it too. A year and 8 months afterwards I stopped Lexapro. It was hard coming down off of it. I had mood swings, depression and a lot of irritability. Whenever I felt bad though, all I'd have to do is look around.

It has now been exactly two years. I couldn't wait to come back from Christmas break and start this new semester. I'm taking a SCUBA diving class and over spring break we're going to go diving in the Bearing Sea. I couldn't wait to go snow skiing, watch the Yukon Quest and the Iditarod, see the International Ice Carving competition, stare at the Aurora and feel that bubble of wonder and excitement rise up in me. And I couldn't wait to see my boyfriend again. We had met randomly, at the Solstice Festival that very first summer I was up here. As fate would have it he is also from Texas and in a spur of adventurous feelings also decided to make Alaska his home away from home while in college. I'm not going to lie. It was hard at first. It was hard wondering if I would be able to have a normal relationship, if he would accept the extra baggage. He accepted them with open arms and our relationship has blossomed into something extraordinary.

Understand that if you are raped or some other horrible act happens to you, I'm not saying moving to the other side of the continent is the solution to all your troubles or that it will only take two years for you to grow into a stronger and better person. But, I do think checking in with yourself and finding out what it is you want and where you want to be is key. Finding people that will support you and love you no matter what comes in as a close second. Reaching out for help is OK and will make things a lot easier. Learning that if you don't like the situation you're in, it can be changed. Kindness from strangers and acquaintances is always appreciated and there is always someone, somewhere in the world that is reaching out their hand to yours. You just need to recognize it.

My Spirit Lives
By Roxanne Chinook

The Nightmare

I close my eyes and lean my head out of the passenger window to feel the warm wind on my face. I do not know who is driving the car as I travel down a familiar canyon road. It is a highway in Idaho- some road that I may have hitchhiked on my way to visit my mother. The car begins to slow down, and when I open my eyes I notice a row of cars with over a dozen young men standing beside them. As we come closer, I feel an overwhelming sense of fear in every cell of my body. The car moves in slow motion as it goes by the row of cars and men. From the beginning to the end of the long row, I notice their faces and recognize each and every one of them. Yet I do not understand why I am so scared. Their faces are smug or unsmiling.

I recognize the cars, but can't remember where I've seen their faces before. Suddenly this roaring noise goes off in my head. I hear this loud popping bang and see this white light. My eyes abruptly open and I realize that I am in my bed. I am unable to move because my entire body is frozen in fear; tears emerge as I realize that all these young men were men that raped me.

Before The Relapse

I am a proud tribal member of the Confederated Tribes of the Warm Springs Indian Reservation, a professional artist and a college graduate. In 1991, I was listed in the 14th Addition of the National Dean's List for receiving a 4.0 while doing postgraduate studies at Boise State University. I was the former Exhibits Coordinator of my tribal museum, and have held several professional positions in the social service field on my reservation. I have three beautiful daughters. My oldest was taken away from me when she was just 14 months old, and raised by very loving and wonderful family in Warm Springs. I was raising my two youngest on my own until my illnesses took them away from me in February 1997.

I stand proud today because I am finally healing from my primary illness, post-traumatic stress disorder (PTSD), and secondary illness, substance abuse. My spirit has been broken many times as a result of these illnesses, which are directly related to the incest and multiple rape wounds of my past. The damage caused by these traumas sought to destroy my very being.

Although I did spend a year or two in recovery since 1979, the first time I experienced real long-term recovery began in Boise, Idaho on August 15, 1987. In 1989, I married a man I met in the early period of my recovery; we had a child together. However, because he battered me I divorced him. In 1991, I moved back to my reservation to work, raise my two daughters, and live near my family. I had abstained from alcohol and cocaine for almost eight years before I relapsed in April 1995.

The Relapse

Since the early 1980's, I have suffered from muscle tension-headaches, extreme anxiety, and depression. However, soon after I moved back to my reservation, I began to experience rape flashbacks, nightmares, insomnia, body numbness, and suicidal thoughts. These symptoms became worse and started to affect all aspects of my life. At times, I felt I was going crazy. I finally sought counseling, but I needed something stronger to relieve my anguish. After almost five years of suffering, I went back to my old coping behaviors and took my first drink in April 1995.

It was not long before I started my new drug of choice, cocaine. I believe it was because the high was more intense than alcohol and I could remain alert. Despite its increased lethality, I was never raped while high on cocaine. I became addicted to cocaine again and found myself on a down hill swirl into darkness. My attempts to recover included everything from counseling, church to taking different medications.

I started to lose everything I gained during my years of abstinence: my self-respect, job, home, car, my relationship with my family. Most important, my children were losing their Mommy, I could not stop the path I was on, and I had not a clue that all these symptoms were interrelated and symptomatic of *rape trauma syndrome.*

The Chicken or the Egg

I had been diagnosed with chronic post-traumatic stress syndrome in the past, and at the time I found some relief having a name for my distress. Nevertheless, my addiction was already in control. So how does one address these kinds of issues when they inevitably trigger the return of substance abuse?

Today I realize that it does not matter which came first, the chicken or the egg. The abuse and my addictions both went hand and hand. I have since learned that for me to refrain from returning to substance abuse, I must address my past traumas.

My victimization began in early childhood when our non-Native grandfather molested my sister and me. His selfish violation of our childhood directly led to the lost of my virginity on a date rape at age 19. I know today that this past trauma kept me from developing appropriate boundaries, self-worth, and basic trust of my own instincts.

I drank so I would not feel or remember. And as my alcoholism progressed, I became more vulnerable to rape. At the time, I did not know why I drank the way I did. Today I know that booze, and later cocaine, became my only means of survival.

The Rapes

Thus, my victim cycle emerged. I was raped 13 times between the ages of 19 and 28. Four of those were gang rapes. One of the rapists was Native American, another Hawaiian mixed, and four were African American, the rest were young white men. I was always extremely intoxicated before the rapes, and could only remember bits and pieces prior to each one, but had very clear memories afterwards. Three of the rapes (one of them a gang rape) happened in Madras, Oregon, a small town just outside my reservation, and the place I made my first and last attempt to seek justice in 1981.

The rape occurred after I was offered a ride back to Warm Springs by a non-Native local man, who was drinking in the same bar I was. He said that he was a friend of my ex-boyfriend, and I thought he was a nice guy. On the drive home he took a detour off the road before the grade goes down to Warm Springs. He pulled the car over and raped me.

After he was done, he acted like nothing was wrong and said no one would believe me anyway. He actually had the audacity to drop me off where I was living. I called the Warm Springs police department only because my brother was a tribal policeman at the time. This incident was the first time that I had the courage to report it. My brother, who happened to be on duty, chased and apprehended him on the flats between Madras and Warm Springs. The rapist was no longer on tribal land, so the Jefferson County police took over and held him in custody overnight.

The next day I went to the Jefferson County police station only to pick up the evidence: my beaded belt and torn bra the officers found in his car. I decided not to press charges because while I was being questioned, the officer told me that it was my word against his, and the rapist told him that the sex was consensual. The Officer also stressed that the rapist had a wife and children to support. I left the police station that day with my head held down in shame, and walked to the nearest bar, never to pursue justice again.

The Shame

It was not long before my whole essence became a warehouse of shame. I was on a road to self-destruction, and became an expert at drowning each incident down with booze that I thought no one would ever suspect what had happened to me. Deep down inside I blamed myself and felt I deserved the abuse. During periods of recovery, I told only a few therapists, counselors, and close friends. I have only recently been able to disclose the number of times I've been raped to others.

Today, when I openly share the amount of times I've been raped, it not only takes away the rapists' power, but also alleviates some of the shame. I also know in my heart that no one deserves to be raped, regardless of the shape they are in.

The Addiction

After my relapsing in April of 1995, I went into treatment in April 1996. But I relapsed within a month after I returned to Warm Springs. My drug of choice was very accessible at the time, and sometimes all it took was one call or unexpected visit from one of my using buddies. In addition, one of the former gang rapists worked at the Indian Health Service, and I did not realize that he was a constant trigger of my PTSD symptoms.

The Suicide Attempt

My family eventually intervened, and my daughters were taken away from me. I do not think I ever experienced so much shame and utter hopelessness in my life. On the evening of February 28, 1997, I unsuspectingly came home while my daughters were packing some clothes to take to my family's house next door. I silently watched as they left - full of disgust for me. I was still coming down from alcohol and cocaine and became overwhelmed with shame and all the pain I caused in my life and in their lives.

I truly wanted to die. The pain was so unbearable that I impulsively took all my antidepressants and called my pastor. I was comatose and hospitalized for three or four days, and was sent directly from the hospital to Oregon Science Hospital (OSH) in Portland for evaluation. I later learned that I had taken more than a lethal dose of pills.

The Overdose

I was at OSH for a few days when I found out that I could only be legally held for 72 hours. I persuaded them to let me out and left the hospital on March 6, 1997, only to return two days later. When I escaped from OSH, I allowed a stranger to shoot me up with heroin, a drug that I had no resistance to. I had already consumed a combination of alcohol, cocaine and crank, and the big hit of heroin was all it took to overdose me. The stranger than dragged my lifeless body down a few flights of stairs to the alley below and left me there to die. The paramedics later told me that someone probably saw me and called 911. I found out that

I had been dead for five minutes, and by the time the ambulance arrived, my skin was blue and cold. I was injected with the drug Narcon to help neutralize the heroine, but it didn't work. The paramedics then used defibrillation to get my heart pumping. I remember how I reluctantly returned to my body. I believe my Creator sent me back to put an end to the cycle of abuse in my life, in my children's lives, and in their children's lives.

After my two-week stay at OSH, I was invited to stay in Oregon City with a loving family in long-term recovery (This family is my oldest daughter's biological father's family, which I have since adopted as my second family.) I was able to stay clean and sober for several months. Unfortunately, as soon as I returned to my reservation, it was just a matter of days before I relapsed. I finally accepted the fact I was not going to die using. My hell was living my addiction.

My Return

On August 18, 1997, my Creator intervened and my tribe allowed me to receive treatment at Sundown M Ranch in Selah, Washington. I was advised by my counselor to continue with treatment, and I agreed to go to a 60-day transitional treatment program at St. Joseph Recovery House here in Bellingham, Washington. I chose to leave everything, my home and the opportunity to be closer to my children, because I knew deep inside that I could not return to Warm Springs. I could not return because of all the triggers and my family's unfaltering animosity towards me, which was created by my relapse.

The guilt and shame from my relapse slowly lifted. I eventually fell in love with Bellingham-the beautiful scenery and all the new friends that I have gained through treatment and support groups. After I completed the 60-day treatment program, my tribe helped me again by paying the rental deposit for the Towanda Oxford House, which is a clean and sober house for women. I then sought the services of the local Private Industry Council and was given the wonderful opportunity to work while being trained to teach art part time at Northwest Indian College.

However, after I had made it through seven months of sobriety, the

PTSD symptoms were so strong that I was again suicidal. This time the suicidal thoughts were more serious because I was not under the influence of either alcohol or drugs. I found my way to the Domestic Violence and Sexual Assault Services of Whatcom County, and was very lucky to be the first and only recipient of a newly funded program that offered one-on-one counseling with a woman (Shelly Olsen, my first Angel) specially trained in these issues.

On the first visit, Shelly was so concerned about my obvious symptoms she immediately contacted the Whatcom Counseling and Psychiatric Clinic to have me reevaluated. She scheduled a visit right away, and I was finally prescribed a medication by Dr. Anselm Parlatore (my second Angel) that specifically helped to control many of my PTSD symptoms.

My true healing began in my one-on-one counseling. I learned that my mind was able to dissociate during my rapes as a form of protection, but my subconscious mind still remembered, causing my severe flashbacks and nightmares. I learned that my closed body language was prevalent in people who have suffered from both incest and rapes. I also learned that some compulsive behaviors I had developed over the years, from my choice of abusive men to my self-destructive substance abuse, were related to my childhood and young adult rapes.

Internalized Oppression

The realization that my Native American heritage played a significant role in the rapes was extremely agonizing. In America's history of the colonization of Native peoples, rape has been used as a weapon of warfare, ethnic cleansing, humiliation and oppression against us. Native peoples have internalized this oppression and passed it down through the generations. My Native grandmother's shame and oppression was passed down to my mother, who passed it on to me to the point that I blamed myself entirely for everything that happened to me.

An example of how whites use rape as a colonial tool of domination against Native women is in embedded in my memory as a severe flashback. I thank my Creator for allowing me to remember the details only when I was in a safe place.

The Drunken Savage

A few days after I was admitted to the first alcohol and drug treatment center since my relapse began in 1995, a kind nurse found me wandering the halls late at night in a catatonic-like state. I had just experienced one of my worst rape flashbacks, and she held me and let me cry as I explained to her what I remembered. When I was living in Hawaii, I was abducted by a group of young Caucasian military men. They took me to a warehouse building on a military base and repeatedly raped me. After they were done, they were concerned about letting me go so they inserted a tall, full bottle of beer inside me to flush their semen out. Throughout the gang rape, they called me derogatory names. One of the rapists asked what might happen if they broke the bottle inside me. An apathetic voice responded, "Who cares? She's nothing but a drunken Indian whore."

In this incident and in the one in Madras, in which the police officer discouraged me from pressing charges against the white male that raped me, it is clear that rape continues to be a tool of domination against Native women.

It's Not My Fault

After several months of working with my counselor, I finally gained the courage to attend Domestic Violence and Sexual Assault Services of Whatcom County's 12-week sexual assault program. This group was very empowering because, for the first time I was able to share my story, in absence of feeling judged or ashamed, with a group of women who were also survivors of traumatic sexual assaults. I also grew to understand that the lifetime of victimization was not my fault and, most of all, I learned that I do not have to be ashamed anymore. Then I moved into the Opportunity's Council's the Dorothy Place, a transitional housing complex for women and children survivors of domestic violence, and was surrounded by brave women who were taking the steps needed in order to break their cycles of abuse and violence.

In 1999, I began the Master of Education in Art program at Western Washington University, and graduated in December 2000, with a cumulative 3.80 GPA. Currently, I am the Director of a nonprofit Art

Marketing Program located at Northwest Indian College.

I now know it was my Creator who sent me back to heal by sharing my story with other survivors and as a way to validate their pain. It was to let them know that they no longer have to feel the deep-rooted shame because they were drunk or high when they were raped. It was to educate professionals in the alcohol and drug treatment field on how important it is to address these issues before the cycle escalates, as well as to be a consultant in the development of new programs that would help survivors heal through artistic expression.

The Re-victimization

During this time I was also fighting to regain custody of my youngest daughter, who was placed with her father, the man I divorced in 1990 because of domestic violence.

I decided to share this part of my struggle because, unfortunately, it is quite common for families to blame and re-victimize survivors. This often happens out of denial and the family's need for the survivor to maintain their social identity as the scapegoat. In addition, as the dually diagnosed family member, I constantly felt their frustration over the years.

My brother, who is a Tribal Judge, and his wife, who works for Children Protective Services, had understandable contempt and anger towards me. Further, during my relapse I had exposed a past deception and, in retaliation, they used their influence to assure that my youngest daughter's father maintained custody of her, despite knowing his history of violence. I do not deny the effect my relapse had on my daughters or my family, and I take full responsibility for this. Nevertheless, professionals I contacted informed me that if I were living anywhere else when my relapse occurred, I would never have lost permanent custody of my girls.

I believe it was because of my brother's abuse of power in the tribal court system that made it impossible for my voice to be heard by an objective ear. However, I did not give up. I made phone calls, sent hundreds of letters and e-mails to domestic violence, child abuse, rape, incest, civil liberties, tribal and state law organizations nationwide. I received dozen of responses, referrals, validations, and kind words of support, but basically referred me back to each other.

The Idaho Coalition Against Sexual and Domestic Violence contacted me to ask permission to use part of my story when the National Organization for Women addressed congress for the re-authorization of the Violence Against Women Act. Edna M. Frantela, from the National Coalition Against Domestic Violence, also asked permission to share my story at a Safe Child Summit, in hopes of effecting the judicial decision-making process regarding high-conflict custody disputes. I was happy that my story might be of some help to other survivors, yet time was running out as my daughter began sharing more abuse she experienced from her father.

Just as I was about to give up all hope my Creator sent my third Angel. Her name is Terilynn Steele, and she founded For The Children Advocacy in California. Having read one of my messages on a tribal-law clearinghouse message board, she wrote me a series e-mail messages of care and support, which renewed my hope. Soon after, my fourth Angel, Lynn Thompson, arrived. She, too, responded to my desperate cry for help after reading a message I left on another tribal law message board. Miraculously, Lynn is not only a Native sister, but also a tribal legal advocate in Idaho. These two women became my angels on earth because they were the only people who were actually willing to do something beyond referring me to another agency. Lynn volunteered her services by preparing my second appeal, which was granted after the tribal court raised my child support in my absence. This allowed the Tribal Court of Appeals to finally hear my case, and these wise men and women eventually validated me and recognized the injustice my daughters and I had endured because of my brother's influence.

Please understand that I don't blame my family for giving up on me; they witnessed my on-and-off self-destructive behaviors over the years. They were genuinely and understandably concern for my children's safety. However, I believe their anger, lack of knowledge, and my brother's retaliation should never have taken precedence over what was in the best interest of my children.

Ending the Cycle of Violence

Though I am still estranged from my brother and his family, today I realize that for me to release victim consciousness, I must learn to embrace forgiveness. My oldest daughter, now 24, is living with me, and working on her associates degree at Northwest Indian College. She is determined to heal from the cycle of abuse and addiction that I passed down to her. No words can describe how very proud I am of her courage to stop the cycles before they take over her life.

My 21-year-old daughter is now in her senior year at a university in Oregon. She is an honor roll student and their track team's number one pole-vaulter. I will always be grateful that my brother and his wife took care of her during her last year of high school. This decision resulted from verbal sexual abuse she experienced from her father, whom the tribal court and Children Protective Services earlier had recommended and granted permanent custody. Even though she was born and raised on my reservation, she is not an enrolled tribal member; unlike me, she has never received tribal financial aid for her higher education. She has worked hard to pay her own way and plans to attend nursing school after she graduates. Again, words cannot describe how proud I am of her courage and inner strength.

My youngest daughter is now 14 years old and has been with me for over two years. We are understandably very close and I am proud to say that she prefers to stay at home creating art to hanging out at the mall with friends. She is my mainstay.

All my daughters are true inspirations and have endured the effects of my past cycle of violence, victimization, and substance abuse. They also bear witness to the changes I have made in my life toward my healing and recovery. I hope they will come to understand the priceless gift I have been given and how my healing will someday help them and their children.

Blaming the Victim

I ask not for sympathy, but for your willingness to understand. This understanding is not just for me, but also for the countless women and children who are sexually abused and raped. I know some people still think that women who drink and use drugs deserve to be raped. Yet the majority of the so-called hopeless alcoholics and addicts, both women and men found repeatedly in alcohol and drug treatment centers, psychiatric hospitals and state and tribal courtrooms, are survivors of childhood traumas such as emotional and/or physical abuse, incest and rape. It continues to horrify me about our society that rape is still tolerated and is an accepted consequence for drinking by women. A female cousin from my reservation laughed as she blamed a Native sister for being gang raped at a party, saying it was her own fault for getting so drunk.

My Healing Journey

By disclosing the many times I have been raped, I continue to erase any debris of shame left inside and pray my disclosure will help other women to break their silence. My continued recovery, the healing I have been able to accomplish with counseling and through my art, is all part of my journey toward resolution.

Much work remains for me to do and I will always have remnants of these horrid traumas, but they will no longer have the power to control my life or define my being.

My Spirit Lives

Reaching this point in my life has taken me years of self-destruction-up to 10 alcohol induced suicide attempts, 6 inpatient treatment centers, 4 outpatient treatment centers, 3 psychiatric hospitals, and several relationships with abusive men. No one should ever have to suffer alone in silence and shame. My grandfather's rape of my childhood led to all the sexual assaults and abuse I experienced in my life. It all started with him, but it ends now. I am not at fault, yet I am responsible. I have returned from a living hell and have found a new purpose in life. Healing is where my spirit lives.

March 2007, Newest Update: My adventurous oldest daughter will be married to a wonderful man in July 2007, and my ambitious middle daughter, has provided my first grandchild! My youngest daughter, a gifted artist, will be graduating from high school this year.

I first published my story in: Social Justice, A Journal of Crime,

Conflict & World Order, and republished in the Annual Editions 06/07 and 07/08, Drugs, Society, and Behavior, McGaw Hill Contemporary Learning Series. Because, "More than 17 million women have been raped in their life, according to a U.S. Department of Justice report for 2006 Native women reported the highest number of rapes of any racial or ethnic group in the United States - a rate 2.5 times higher than the national average," all of these venues, and the development of a presentation - training based on my story research titled, My Spirit Lives, Helping to End the Cycle of Multiple Rape and Substance Abuse for Native Women and Women of Color, has allowed me to educate and reach more people and survivors. This is how my spirit lives today!

Pretty Ones

It's the pretty ones

that age so quickly,

sitting on the same barstool

day after day she tries not to remember.

At first her youth and beauty

captivates an admiring audience

but they too,

wonder what will happen

when her beauty begins to fade.

The jealous ones

try to cut her,

scar her pretty face,

but no one could imagine

the scars she already has.

It's the pretty ones,

they say are lucky,

because she has drinks all lined

up for her.

But there's no one there to protect her,

when she's drunk herself into a stupor,

blinded by all the booze.

Or when they dump her out on the highway,

after her use was put beyond human test.

She walks alone trying to forget

what just happened,

and the shame she feels from being

one of the pretty ones.

She goes back to her barstool.

Roxanne Chinook

(Written just before my relapse in 1995.)

Journey Through Fear
By Sara Ylen

"A life lived in fear is a life half-lived." As those words were spoken to me for the first time at the age of 30, I felt a mixture of inspiration and sorrow. Memories were flooding to the surface and all of them were associated with fear. I choked and fought back tears as I tried to wrestle these recollections into submission but to no avail. The past was going to haunt me forever at this rate. I knew it deep in my soul that day as I struggled to deny my roots. It was time to surrender and go back to the beginning once again....

Flat terrain and infinite fields of corn, navy beans, and sugar beets were the characteristics of my hometown surroundings. Growing up in a small farming community had lent itself to living undetected under the domination of a controlling, violent man I called "Daddy." My mother, a heart patient since birth, had chosen self-preservation over the protection of her children. Her fear gave birth to mine.

"Just wait until your father gets home." I would tremble as those words echoed in my direction, knowing that the peace of death would be preferable to what would happen when my father walked in the door. My earliest memories start at age three and no memory goes untouched by the rage of a man who wanted perfect little soldiers in his repertoire of life accomplishments. Everything seemed to anger him. As a three-year-old I started sleep-walking. Each night I'd wander to an interesting place for the rest of the night's sleep, until one night, I parked across the door-way of my parents' bedroom. My father, an early riser, tripped over me on his way down the darkened hallway. I can still hear the sickening thud and feel the blinding pain as he kicked me down the hallway to the entrance of my own bedroom and left me there. Times like these were far too frequent to recount and each event escalated more than the previous one.

At the age of six, I became caretaker, mother, and substitute wife. Each role fed the voracious fear that raged inside of me. By day, I was cook and cleaning lady. By night, I was captive to the diseased mind of a child molester who would, years later, be profiled as a sexual sadist. I would pray to disappear into the sunset that cast a glow on my bedroom wall while I tried to escape from the sweaty stench of my father breathing in my face and destroying my innocence. What started off as violent rape soon turned into sadistic torture. He had no conscience.

A result of his upbringing, my brother started to follow in our father's footsteps. Being three years my elder, he was my best friend. Dad had isolated us from everyone and my brother was my only companion much of the time. We starved together when mom would sleep all day and demand that we stay in our rooms without food. We would hide outside in the barn together when dad was angry and searching for an outlet. We would find safe havens under bridges and catch crayfish while we pretended to be someone else's children. I respected him more than anyone. We had both been robbed of childhood as we struggled to survive in the traumatic adult world we'd been hurled into.

However, the summer he turned twelve and I was nine, darkness overtook him. That summer, he became his father's son, forcing me into oral sex and organizing times his friends could come over and do what they wanted to his sister. My safety net was gone. I felt abandoned by everyone.

By the time I was fifteen, I had been pregnant twice because of incest. My father would know and he would beat me within inches of death, forcing miscarriage every time. All I wanted was a way out. I had tried telling friends and teachers. Social workers and police officers had questioned my father and me, documenting bruises and pregnancies. Ultimately, the monster won. Time after time, he'd convince everyone I was lying and the saving I hoped for never occurred. My childhood was half-lived. I depended on fear to survive. Those years were the roots of my sorrow.

At the tender age of 18, I married my first love and vowed to never look back. I would rise above my fear, perfect being a wife to a man who deserved my love, and pray for the chance to raise my own children in a home that would be full of unconditional love and acceptance. Fear would not enter into our home or the hearts of my children. For eight blissful years, I enjoyed just such a home. I grew as an individual, fought to leave my childhood in the past, and brought two beautiful sons into the world. Motherhood was everything I'd dreamed it to be and I dedicated my existence to giving my sons health, happiness, and security. I had defeated the cycle of panic and violence and I basked proudly in the peaceful aura that encircled my children.

But fear did not stay banished. It made an undesirable return to my life on May 12, 2001 in the form of a stranger in a parking lot. And this time, my terror would take on a life of its own. I worried I would never be the same. The beauty of it is—I never was.

Saturday, May 12, 2001 was a cliché day—sunny, not a cloud in the sky, and blissfully balmy. By mid-morning, I had been transformed into a beautiful swan by a talented stylist as I described to her the dress I would be wearing for my friend's wedding the next day. My friend had entrusted me with rehearsal dinner details and a polished wedding procession. The dinner was to be that night and I was as energized about it as I was the wedding that would follow the next day. For all intents and purposes, life was perfect. All I needed were a few items from the grocery store and my plans would be complete. So I drove to the busiest, most economical store in the area. There, in that parking lot, as I parked my car, opened my door, and reached back to grab my purse, the clock struck twelve and my beautiful life disappeared.

He was there. I turned and at the same moment, I felt his hand crushing my arm. His smell—the alcohol, the cigarettes, and the foul "all-night-at-the-bar" odor—pierced my brain quickly. He was wasting no time as he continued to crush my arm, pushing against me, swearing at me, and finally laughing as I begged him to take my possessions and let me go. Instead, he invaded every personal space I possessed as he pummeled my unsuspecting body, laughed as I begged for my life, raped me, and left me exposed and unconscious. When consciousness finally returned, I started my long descent into the most dismal era of my life. In that instant, panic and terror had me in a steel grip, compelling me to believe that I would never be able to go on.

In my craving for safety, I drove the 25 plus miles from that parking lot to the home I shared with my husband and little boys. To this day, I have no memory of that drive home. What is etched in my memory, though, is the look on my husband's face when I stepped inside our home and let my full weight fall against our insulated door. I knew from that moment that I could never tell him the whole truth. It would kill him—break his heart—and our children couldn't afford to lose another parent. I felt as if my ability to mother was already shattered. After all, I'd promised my children on the day of their births that I would provide total and absolute protection. How could I protect them, though, when I was living in sheer terror myself?

My inability to face the truth induced denial of gargantuan proportions that allowed me to carry on a beleaguered existence. Though I tried to maintain normalcy, the truth was never far under the surface and little by little, I knew I had to start facing it. I had shared enough of my truth with my husband to explain my physical injuries. So when, 48 hours after my attack, I decided to contact the police, I only shared those same details with the investigating officer. Incident report number in hand, I repeated this performance for the emergency room physician assigned to care for the muscle and nerve damage to my neck, left arm and shoulder, and displaced ribs and pelvic bones.

"Sara, you have to tell your husband." It was the Tuesday after my assault and I had broken my silence over a steak and a baked potato. The steak turned to rubber and my throat closed as my trusted confidante stared into my startled eyes. I had just described to her in sketchy terms the moment before I faded into unconsciousness for the second time, when "the man" had slid his gold nugget and diamond ring onto the knuckle of his middle finger. Through clenched teeth he swore at me and vowed to shut me up as he forced that ring and finger inside my body. She hadn't even heard the most horrible component of my defilement—the second rape. But already, she was making demands. My body was throbbing with pain, my abdomen cramped, and I could smell his scent as nausea washed over me in vicious waves.

"I can't," was my edgy response. However her facial expression spoke volumes and I knew that before the day was over, I would comply. That night, as I struggled to find the words, I reached the same threshold with my husband that I had earlier that day at lunch. I couldn't go beyond that first violation. His reaction to just that portion of my reality was more than either of us could handle. Adrenaline took over as I ran from room to room, locking windows and doors, closing curtains, and making repeated checks that all points of entry were locked and protected. My fear had just escalated into hysteria.

"Do you think I want this to be true? I don't. It would be so much easier...." Pain enveloped my body and cut off my air mid-sentence. I fell to the floor, sobbing. Nighttime settled in and agony became my companion as searing pelvic pain and abnormal bleeding overtook me. By morning, I was begging my husband to return me to the emergency room. I wanted him to believe. I wanted someone to tell me I was going to be okay. I wanted to surrender to the capable hands of a doctor and nurse who understood that rape was a living hell.

No such professional existed, however. Despite my inner pleading, there was no peace or resolution. The doctor and nurse took turns reprimanding me for the egregious mistake of waiting too long to come forward.

"Rape kits are useless past 72 hours, Mrs. Ylen." The word "useless" flashed through my mind like a neon sign. Synonyms inundated my brain—expendable, hopeless, worthless, weak, inadequate, and futile. Yes. Those words seemed accurate. It was time to admit that's what I was. I decided then and there that I would be forever broken.

For several agonizing months, I struggled just to move past the physical wounds I'd been left with. Pain killers and muscle relaxers became my favored companions. I watched my children build their own walls of fear. At night, my four-year-old angel would pray for "the bad man" to leave his mommy alone. As my physical pain slowly started to subside, I was left with the startling reality that the deepest wounds were yet to be faced and that was an impossible task. It meant admitting pain, violation, betrayal, and what those things had done to my self-worth.

"One day at a time, Sara," was everyone's catch phrase as if it carried the cure I was seeking. But one day was too much. One hour was too much. I had to live minute to minute. Nothing else seemed achievable. Each day I woke up in a cloud of despair, feeling abandoned by pretty much everyone in my life, and worrying that my children were being eternally affected by my nagging self-doubt and misery. Life was desultory and meaningless. Inside me something was screaming to get out, but there was no clearly marked exit. Little did I know that it was a warrior who wanted out and the next person I met would name her "Xena."

Thirteen months after my rape, the first of several first-rate police officers came into my life. As a Sergeant for the Michigan State Police and as a survivor of child sexual abuse, she extended an invitation to me if I should ever wish to talk. Expecting that she would scold me as did everyone before her; I contemplated her offer with trepidation. With nothing to lose, I finally walked into her place of employment and started the journey that would turn things around. For two uninterrupted hours, she sat across from me as I stumbled and stammered my way through the telling. I wanted her to understand but my vocabulary didn't include the phrase "I was raped." Finally, she put her hand up and I stopped speaking.

"Sara, you were raped," she said slowly and methodically, letting it pierce my subconscious. "You can't deny that anymore. He got a piece of you. But he didn't get all of you. The pieces that are left are pretty good. So fight for them!"

Fight for them? She spoke with such conviction and fervor that something inside me immediately shifted.

"You can do it, Sara. I will believe in you until you believe in you." Her statements were laconic but her intent was clear. She would be my teacher, instructing me in the highly coveted art of reclaiming myself by going to war for what is rightfully mine.

Within days, my trust in her direction was put to the test. As I drove to a doctor's appointment, I passed a vehicle waiting to pull out in traffic. The driver was a man—one who strongly resembled my attacker. He entered traffic behind me and as my panic-stricken heart raced, I studied this man in my rear view mirror. He raised his left hand to run his fingers through his long hair and on his middle finger was a ring. The pounding in my head kept time with my heart as my body braced for another attack and throbbed in remembrance of the first one. Numb and immobile, I sat in the parking lot of my doctor's office, not knowing how I got there.

"The pieces that are left are pretty good, Sara. Fight for them." Those words echoed through my head as tears started to freely flow. I wanted to fight but I didn't know how. What I did know is that my fear was larger than life and if I did nothing then I would be looking over my shoulder for the rest of my life. I didn't deserve that. More than that, my children didn't deserve that.

My next stop was at my therapist's office where I choked out every facet of my traffic scare and expressed my longing to fight back. Within minutes, I was in my therapist's car heading toward the driveway "he" had pulled out of earlier that morning. Armed with an address, I placed a phone call to the original investigating officer. His shock that I would call him over a year later was unmistakable.

And so my journey through the criminal justice system began. It would be measured in months of peaks and valleys. Four full days would be spent looking through 8,000 mug shots of white males that led to my attacker's undeniable identification, only to fail weeks later at picking him out of a corporal lineup because he'd completely changed his appearance. Outstanding detectives would discover a pawn shop record that led back to the man I identified, verifying he'd pawned a ring matching my description just four days after raping me. Employment records would establish that he was an employee of the store where the crime occurred and that he was at work that fateful day. I provided a description of a skull tattoo on my attacker's right bicep and the man from the mug shot possessed that exact tattoo. The case was inundated with delays but ultimately, in March of 2003, James Eugene Grissom—the man who destroyed pieces of my life—was arrested and charged with two counts of first degree criminal sexual conduct, each bearing up to life in prison as penalty.

New emotions, positive ones, overwhelmed me—feelings of power, security, victory, and freedom. These feelings were ephemeral, though, as I tried to reconcile the desire to see it through with the dread of facing this man in court. Confronted with reliving every grisly, lurid detail in front of a judge and jury, I felt fragmented and uncertain. However, once again what I most feared was the very thing that strengthened and transformed me.

My friend, the Sergeant, had been there through all the ups and downs. She willingly graced me with the benefits of her professional and personal experience and I could feel something decisive growing inside me. As I described each personal battle that arose while waiting for the trial, suddenly a smile spread across her face.

"You've got it, Sara. You found the warrior princess inside you and I, for one, don't want to mess with Xena. So when you feel like you're going to lose it, let Xena take over and you'll be fine."

After numerous pretrial motions and postponements, the felony trial finally started on August 19, 2003. With the help of greatly trusted professionals, I had exerted tremendous effort in preparing myself for testifying. This had to be the moment where I spoke my truth without fearing the man who had created it. I wanted to be real—connected to the pain that I was going to describe—for only then could I truly be heard.

The trial was spread out over a period of eight days and the night before I was going to take the stand, I snuggled with my boys in front of the television. As we watched a movie together, the dialog grabbed hold of my psyche when I heard a character say: "Courage is not the absence of fear, but rather the judgment that there is something more important than fear." The inner halcyon that suddenly set in raised my awareness. This was the answer—courage. I could get through testifying if I decided that telling my truth was more important living in dread.

"Please state your full name for the court and spell your last name." I inhaled sharply as my moment of truth began with this by-the-book exchange. For 2 ½ hours, I bore witness to the gruesome acts committed against me and defied the entrapment of the defense attorney. In the end, the judge and jury saw James Eugene Grissom through my eyes—as a singularly repugnant man. More importantly, as I stepped off the stand and released all of the agony I had been carrying for two years, the truth had set me free. My attacker was in jeopardy and his fear glistened in his eyes and glowed in ghastly white skin. From that point on, I knew there was going to be more than fear in my life. There would be hope. I felt it with every fiber of my being.

Five days after testifying, the trial finally ended. Less than an hour of deliberation sent two "guilty" verdicts echoing through the courtroom. Stepping outside of the courthouse that day, my ebullience peaked and so my journey into healing accelerated. That night, as I celebrated my personal triumph, I hugged my boys tightly. My oldest son saw my perpetual smiles and wondered why I was different.

"You don't have to pray for that bad man to leave me alone anymore, honey. The bad man got told he's going to prison." He threw his arms around me as his own little face lit up.

"For how long, Mommy? Forever?"

"I don't know. The judge will have to decide that in a few weeks."

"I hope he goes to prison for a million-billion-trillion years, Mom."

"Me too, honey. Me too."

Ultimately, the judge rewarded my survival and truth-telling by exceeding the sentencing guidelines and sending my rapist to prison for 15 to 35 years. What a remarkable victory! However, the greater triumph in all of this has been the journey of reclaiming me. I had lived far longer than I wanted to admit, believing that I was worthless. Malevolent shadows had surrounded so much of my life that I was convinced it was all I could lay claim to. However the alchemy of being a rape survivor is that it has the power to make you so much stronger than you can ever imagine—if you let it.

One of my first conversations with a fellow rape survivor had introduced just such a concept. She was four years past her rape and she told me if I just trusted the process, someday I would be grateful for what had happened to me. I rolled my eyes and determined instantly that she was insane. How could someone ever be grateful for violation and betrayal? Now, as I approach the six year anniversary of my rape, I understand.

Life is not merely what happens to you. It is what you carry inside of you as you walk through each moment. I never would have appreciated this if not for my life experiences. For a long time I would repeat the courage mantra from the movie, all the while feeling like courage was fleeting. As I stepped into the public eye and told my personal story so that others might be helped, I heard people refer to me as "brave" and "strong." I rejected those portrayals, not believing that I deserved such honorable titles.

Today, though, I can say "thank you" and know there is more than fear and uncertainty. I have the satisfaction of knowing that I have fought battles in the past two years that I never would have approached, were it not for the experience that caused my personal awakening. Triumphantly, I have fought back even against my father. He knows, now, that I will not be silent any longer. Though he remains a free man instead of a condemned criminal, I take steps every day to be free of the memories that haunt me. Each sadistic trauma he inflicted is a measurement of who he is—not who I am. They are pieces of me. They don't define me.

Even now, I battle cancer that threatens to destroy me. But I will not live half of a life because of fear. Surrender is no longer an option. What I now carry inside me is hope, determination, and peace—the hope that I will be able to keep learning, the determination to be true to what is important, and the peace of knowing that my children will never again lose their mother to a madman. E. E. Cummings said it best when saying this: "To be nobody-but-yourself—in a world, which is doing its best, night and day, to make you everybody else—means to fight the hardest battle which any human being can fight; and never stop fighting."

The Grey
© By Sara Ylen 2006

It's not in the white that you really think, Nor is it in the black. It washes over me as I peer into the gray. For in the white, all seems well. The gray is hidden, and the brightness Makes me grin and close my mind. And in the black...I cannot dare to look. It is what I do not want to see. It reigns in the shadows of my soul. Out of fear I turn my back. But when I dip into another realm, Such as October in the evening, The sky is one even cloud, and the world is cold and gray. The bare trees bend, and dead leaves rustle with angry wind. It is a very ghastly calm, But this is when I can truly see. It is not so black that I run away, Nor is it so white that I look past it. It is where I can rethink things. It is on these days when I ponder As I gently swing in the park, Revisited by my haunting thoughts. Of the white and of the black, This is when I can only see What truly lies within me. It is hidden in the eerie gray That dwindles and totters... And soon washes away.

This Brick Is Not Mine
Kareema S. Griest
9/6/03 ©

These walls that were built
To protect my heart
Were built on lies, anger and guilt
With pain and suffering thrown into the mix
You helped me build them
One brick at a time
Without moving at all
They've been my stronghold –
My "fortress" if you will –
Against the rest of the world around me
They wouldn't let anyone in
But they didn't let me out
Holding back all my emotions and memories
Until the day you came to say
That you were sorry
Sorry for not believing me
Sorry for the pain that was caused
And suddenly the walls were in a shambles
The flood gates opened up from Hell
And stormed past my resistance
To tear these walls down to rubble
And now I'm left beneath to sort through
What's left of all of my walls
What's this? Lies told to me ~
That brick is not mine,
But fear ~ oh, yeah ~ that one is…
Deceit, blame, anger, and hatred towards me ~
Those aren't my bricks either
Suddenly, there are bricks
That are broken and shattered
Like tiny shards of glass
I need to get through these bricks

To rebuild my walls of safety
But this time, they won't be so high
I'll allow others in,
But these walls will remind me
To be careful with my heart
(These bricks are not all mine...)
Now here are all *your* bricks
(These bricks are not all mine...)
The ones I don't want or need
Take them back to your own walls of Hell
(These bricks are not all mine...)
For you will never have the same
Hold on me ever again
The truth is out now
And you have finally seen
That YOU were in the wrong...NOT ME!
These bricks are not all mine...
And now it's time for me to heal...

Never Again

Never again will I give you

Ultimate power over me
Never again will I allow you
To cause me so much pain
Never again will I let you
Get away with the things that you do
Never again will I tolerate
Your insults, cruelty and threats
Never again will you be able
To keep me under your thumb
Never again will you control my life,
Degrade me or make me feel dumb
Never again will I believe you
When you tell me I'm not good enough
Never again ~ never again ~ never, ever again
For I am finally free of you
The choices in my life will be _mine_

I will be whomever _I_ choose to be

And learn to love myself again
I am no longer a fragile, empty shell
Always ready to break
I am alive, full of courage and hope
And stronger than you think
Your words and hands can no longer hurt me
For _I_ am the one now in control
And you are the one who is weak
Without all my fears to feed upon
You have nothing else left
Now I have a journey ahead of me
One that may seem I can't bear
But it is one I will take on gratefully
For it means I will no longer follow

Anything else but what's in my heart
This heart that has been shattered and lost –
A heart I thought did not even exist –
Has finally started to beat again
It's no longer the heart of a victim
That's afraid to face the world on its' own
It's a heart that will never let hatred win
For – to fear – I will never again give in

Never again ~ never again ~ never, ever again

Kareema S. Griest 9/11/02

Victim Impact Statement
Anne Heck

Victim is not a word I use to describe myself. Even then, I viewed myself as athletic, strong, perhaps even invincible. My rape came as a surprise. I was aware of rape, but it was one of those experiences I had never imagined being part of my own life.

That was the summer of 1990 and my case, until recently, remained unsolved. In January of 2004, through an unusual series of events, the National DNA database identified the man who raped me. In preparation for a trial and sentencing, I was asked by the prosecuting attorney to put into words my statement about the impact of this incident. Victim I was not. Impacted I was.

Impact aptly describes much of my experience. There was the initial impact of his fist hitting my face, the impact of him throwing my bike into the bushes, the impact of his body forcing itself into mine. Then there were the blazing sirens that delivered me to the hospital, my body becoming the source of evidence, my swollen face in the mirror, and the pain in friends' faces.

But there was something much deeper. Now, 14 years later, I was faced with the task of communicating this impact; it was not easily put into words.

Statement—my statement—a declaration to the court of how this incident has affected my life. I played with the idea for three months. How could I share the impact of this heinous crime without participating in the role of victim? How could I focus on the positive outcomes without minimizing the act?

Once I became clear on my questions, I was gifted with answers. One afternoon in April as I spoke with the District Attorney, he shared with me the story of the other woman, raped just one day prior by the same man who had escaped from a road gang of prisoners working in West Virginia. She was relaxing on her porch swing. She, too, was hit in the face, raped, and her car was stolen. Her young daughter witnessed the act and managed to climb on a stool to reach the kitchen phone and dial 911; she then hid in the closet.

The words struck deeper than replaying my own drama. It hit some emotional treasure chest that released some long-held gifts. This story gave me the opportunity to view myself with true compassion. It also enabled me to open my heart to receive just the words I needed to express.

The following is my **Victim Impact Statement**, submitted to Prince William County Office of the Commonwealth's Attorney in June 2004. It was read in court at the sentencing on October 29 of that same year.

I was raped in July 1990. It was a beautiful summer day and I was enjoying a road trip on my bicycle exploring back roads. I loved the freedom I felt on two wheels with the sun on my back. What a stark contrast this incident was to my intention for that day.

As one can expect, this crime has had a huge impact on my life. Without this experience, I feel I would have missed out on much of the richness available in life. While I don't believe this richness need come only when faced with adversity, I do believe this horrific event provided a background of contrast that created a more vivid palette for my life. At age 40 and 14 years beyond this event I can honestly say that I'm grateful for the growth that this path has provided me.

While I do not condone Mr. McDonald's act and feel he should receive his just sentence, I have come to accept this as a chapter of my life that has provided me with the potential for my personal healing and development.

There are many facets of this growth that I believe serve witness to the impact this rape has had on my life and I'd like to share a few of those:

The day I was raped, I learned about friendship and kindness when a stranger picked me up along that dusty road and took me crumpled and terror-stricken to the closest paramedic unit. A rather new acquaintance made calls to dentists for me. I had two teeth that were knocked out of place and a kind doctor agreed to stay late to help me. Unfortunately, the teeth were irreparable, the roots damaged. I would eventually have to have root canals and other reparative work done to them.

I learned about letting go as I had my favorite blue biking shorts and shirt, stained with blood, bagged by police and taken away for evidence.

I grew into new ways of viewing my freedom as I had my trusty touring bike covered in black fingerprint dust returned to my apartment. It sat untouched for weeks.

I remember with disgust the volunteer at the hospital who came into my room to read scripture and tell me I could be forgiven for my sins. I experienced what it felt like to be shunned at the health center when I went in for a pregnancy test and shared that I had been raped. I quickly learned to trust my own knowing that I had done nothing wrong.

A dear friend of mine drove to see me the day after the rape; he loaded me in his car and drove me to my parents' home. My parents were mostly silent, unable themselves to process the emotion of what had happened. I learned that those who love you often have the hardest time expressing their hurt to you.

At the beginning I remember with some fuzziness passing many days in deep fear, jumping at the smallest sounds, panicking at daybreak, dizzy from my lack of breath, unable to face crowds or put myself in the presence of strangers. I learned to give credence to my intuition and listen to my body.

Months passed and I had the opportunity to participate in group and personal counseling, both of which I abhorred as it was extremely challenging to get to the emotion of my experience when that emotion was mostly trapped in my body. I learned patience with process and had the opportunity to look closer at my own character.

I woke many nights with a vivid picture of the perpetrator in my head and often drew pictures of him hoping that putting it on paper would somehow purge my body of my relentless fearful thoughts and feelings. This taught me to let my emotions flow through me.

I learned about patience and trust as I waited 10 days to receive the results of my HIV test. I experienced my lack of readiness for learning self-defense when I broke into uncontrolled tears at my first class; I learned how to be kind to myself.

After several more months, I did complete a self-defense class that allowed me to release lots of the emotion I had packed in my body. My women colleagues where I taught high school all came to support me at my graduation. I learned how deeply all women are affected by acts of rape and abuse and I learned wherever women come together, there is intense power that can be created.

A year after my rape, I left Manassas, hoping to leave my intense emotions behind and find a more peaceful environment in which to heal. Initially panic set in and I gradually learned how to build a support system for myself. I had the good opportunity to find a wonderful group of supporters at a local Rape Crisis Center whom I called on periodically when my body was remembering the trauma and my mind didn't know how to process it.

After much more counseling and lots of tears, I undertook training as an Advocate at the Rape Crisis Center and also served on their Speaker's Bureau. There I learned how very many women shared my horror and I learned how to respond appropriately to those who were healing as well as those who had never experienced rape.

Within a couple of years, I had received training in women's self defense from a number of programs and began teaching assertiveness training to young women. I had great passion for the topic and quit my teaching position at a local high school to devote my time fully to this endeavor. Through this I gained confidence and strength and a deep admiration for women.

As time has passed, I have thought about that horrid day less and less. What had remained until, actually less than two months ago, was a persistent and often severe pain in my pelvis and hips. This pain began in the year following the rape and has been my most constant reminder that there was emotion that had still not been released – my body's reminder that I still had some growing to do.

I have met with all types of medical, psychological and alternative health professionals over the years, always hoping to find the path that would relieve my pain. I've gone through too many months of feeling tired and frustrated from this drain in energy and weeks of being unable to walk.

This past January, I declared this my year of strength. Within a week after that declaration, I received a phone call from Detective Newsome sharing the developments in a case that I had felt would go unsolved. I knew then that my dream to feel whole was soon to be fulfilled.

I have two young children now who are vibrant with life's energy and I've longed to experience my own peak health and fully enjoy my time with them. Indeed, I'm ready for that piece of growth that provides me my freedom.

The time for that growth is now and my intent for participating in this sentencing is to close this chapter of my life, to release whatever negative emotion I may still be holding in my body and to feel the freedom and joy that I so clearly had that morning 14 years ago when I left home to enjoy a day of biking.

Some people tell me I'm courageous for appearing in court. I believe I'm blessed to have the opportunity to experience this part of my healing process. This event is for me a symbolic statement of hope fulfilled and justice served and most importantly, it demonstrates the power of choosing my own strength.

On August 23, 2004, Terry L. McDonald, who was serving a 48-year sentence for sexual assault in West Virginia, pleaded guilty in Prince William County, Virginia Circuit Court to rape and abduction with intent to defile. The Judge in this case was asked to give McDonald the maximum punishment—two life terms in prison—at his October 29 sentencing.

I returned to Virginia on the sentencing date to read this statement to the court. I took my bike and declared my freedom on those dusty back roads in Virginia.

Dedicated to: My Savior who heard my cries and healed my heart; my amazing parents who held my hand while I screamed through my pain; Sister Marjorie who told me to, "go home, tell the Lord how I feel and this is when the healing will come;" my college roommate who sat beside me and stroked my hair while I sobbed into my pillow; and my wonderful husband who honors my past and chooses to walk beside me into the future.

My Story...I thought it would stay there where I left it, burning in the toilet, an exercise that felt so freeing, but it continues to demand attention. I suppose that is how it goes when something in life comes full circle.

I've binged my story. I've vomited my story in ally ways. I've starved my story and landed in rehab. I've exercised my story in an attempt to run from it. I've taken boxes of laxatives at a time to excrete my story to the point of passing out. I've smoked my story in Bible College. As an adult I have hidden under desks from my story. I've screamed my story into the ocean waves. I've wailed my story into the darkness of night. I've cried my story until I fell to sleep. Finally, I am telling my story. I have been ashamed of my story but now I am proud of it because it no longer terrorizes me at night. It no longer robs me of a beautiful life. I am proud to say I have overcome what I experienced!

The first time I knew something was wrong was when I was about seven years old. My Aunt presented me with a Christmas gift. I tore the paper and opened the box to find a frilly little girls' nightgown. Suddenly I felt as if my heart sank into my stomach and was strangely overwhelmed with shame. I had no idea what was happening but I knew I was afraid of my feelings and had to get away from that nightgown. I felt embarrassed by my reaction because I did not understand it.

Jump to eight years later when I was struggling with anorexia and bulimia to the point of suicide. I lived daily feeling such unexplainable shame and guilt, trying to numb myself by controlling my body. My days went in cycles of starvation and exercise to binging and trying to vomit. Truly I have lost count of the amount of times I found myself eating out of the garbage can in a mad attempt to numb my terrifying feelings. One such day I was laying on the floor in my bedroom looking at old pictures when I came across one of myself around age four dressed in a pretty little pink nightgown. I starred frozen at the picture. Horrified, I ran to the bathroom and sat in front of the toilet. My mind was confused and my body felt all sorts of invasive sensations. I began wailing as I remembered myself as that little girl in the pretty pink nightgown and the teenage boy next door who use to babysit me. I felt so dirty and ashamed. I can only explain it as an overwhelming feeling of ickiness. That feeling had always been with me up to that point but now I was beginning to make a connection. I was remembering. A few weeks later I packed my bags and headed off to the Renfrew Center for Eating Disorders in Philadelphia. It was at the Renfrew Center that my newly acquired vice of smoking really began to mature. It sort of helped numb out some of the pain that came up during my therapy sessions. I jumped into a world I had never known before. The youngest of about thirty women age nineteen to around sixty, I heard stories and could relate to experiences in ways I never had before. Really no further memories of abuse came to me until fifteen years later, but I am jumping ahead.

Fresh out of rehab I moved to a new state and felt like a stranger in a foreign land. New places always take a period of adjustment but especially for a teenager who felt she had some terrible secret to hide. Where I came from I was one of many working through an eating disorder. Where I moved to no one seemed to pay any attention to that sort of thing. I was a loner. Perhaps I could have made friends my age but I felt so far beyond my peers because of the path my life had taken that I was certain they could not relate to me. I became active in a local church and at seventeen I was involved in the college and young adult Bible groups. It was in this environment where I met the man who would manipulate and rape me for about a year.

A counselor at a local psychiatric hospital, my rapist was about twenty-four years old, large, heavy, and rather commanding in his demeanor. He was interested in me. He liked me. I can still remember him coming to see me at my part time job at the GAP. I had never received attention like this from a man and found it nice. I had no friends. Not one. Our group went on a church retreat to a camp ground in the woods. That night while everyone enjoyed hayrides he and I wandered off to a playground.

We sat on swings, went down slides and talked. He began asking me very personal questions. Intimate relational questions. I thought he really cared for me. Looking back I know he was trying to find his angle with me. He led me to an old barn up to a hay loft. I followed him. That was when it began. That is where it should have ended. Some could say it was my fault for having put myself in that position. I should have known better. What was a seventeen year old girl doing in a barn with a grown man? I carried that guilt and shame for years. I do not carry it anymore! But to this day I find myself trying to make sense of how it went so far that I was no longer in control. Then I have to remind myself I lost control the moment we wandered from the group.

The next night I was home and thought I had a new boyfriend in this guy. What a thought! My parents were out and he came over. He came up to my room and sat on my bed. Again I don't remember how it happened but it happened and he went further this time. I didn't know what to do. I do remember feeling like I could not leave where I was. I was frozen but I could not explain why I felt that way. Then he left. That was it. I felt numb, dirty, ashamed like I had a bad secret to keep. I started binging and purging almost right away. The next day he asked me over to his house. I do not remember all of what happened but I do know that was the first time he tried to penetrate me. This began a sick and abusive cycle, month after month for almost a year. The more I saw him the worse it got. He treated me like an animal. Even now, as I write, I toy with the ideas of why I felt I was so worthless and why I gave him that kind of power over me. It was the perfect cycle of destruction for who I was at the time—alone, worthless in my eyes, and friendless. This guy seemed to 'care' for me. He abused me. Afterward he showed me some attention and then he abused me again...it got worse and worse each time as I plunged to lower levels of shame. I was stuck. What could I do? Who could I tell? How could I make it end? He called me. He looked for me. How could I break free?

Finally I could not take the shame of all that was happening, so I told my mother. I cried and cried because of how dirty I felt. No matter what I did or how hard I tried to numb out of reality I could not escape the filth I felt all over my body. He called my house looking for me and wanted me to come and take a 'nap' with him. I knew what that meant so I declined and made an appointment with a clergy member at my church. My mother came with me and I actually told the pastor we had been 'sexually active.' How is this possible that a young teenage girl would call the dirty perversion of all that happened 'sexually active?' I felt such blame, fault, humiliation, and shame. That is all I thought I was worth. The pastor arranged a meeting for both of us at his office. My rapist carried a file into the meeting and handed it to the pastor. He proceeded to say he hardly knew me and had no idea where I got my story but had prepared a psychological analysis of my personality in his defense. He informed the pastor that I was stalking him and showed up at his parents home without an invitation at one time. He continued saying he was sure he was not the first person I had been with (little point that seemed to go unnoticed!). He continued on but at this point I just stared at him in disbelief and sort of zoned out. When he finished rambling the pastor looked at me and I said, 'I have to stand before God someday and I have told you the truth.' It was in that moment that I knew I would not press charges. What would have been the point? What evidence did I have? I was too ashamed to even call it rape at this point. Instead I fell deeper into bulimia and went back into treatment. A few months later I left for college. I moved half way across the country to try and escape this man, his friends and my pain.

Who was I kidding? Running never solves anything. Little did I know I was about to fall to such depths of pain using bulimia to try and cope. I lied to people. I stole food. I hoarded laxatives. In my vain attempt to purge the filth and shame I felt I took boxes laxatives at a time. Some pills were orange, some yellow, others white, but they all had that funny aftertaste and smooth nauseating feeling sliding down the back of my throat. One by one I remember punching them out of their foil compartments and washing them down with Diet Coke before bed. I would binge on seven thousand calories. Seven thousand was the key number because then I knew to starve myself as, 'punishment' for six days. Only one thousand calories a day. Easy to calculate. Usually around 2AM the rumbling began—the stabbing pains in my abdomen and back, stabbing and stabbing until I would run to the bathroom in my dorm and sit down just in time. Forty minutes I would sit and it would just keep coming and my shame would start to go away – I was numbing out emotionally. Forty minutes I would sit and still it would come. My legs would go numb from sitting, my feet touching the icy cold tile floor. I felt so tired, so weak, I just wanted to sleep, to escape. Finally I was finished. I can remember standing up and falling to my knees because I was dizzy. I would crawl to my bed and fall back to sleep for maybe fifteen minutes and then I would head to the bathroom again. All night this would go on until around 7AM. My roommate left for class and I rolled over too weak to get out of bed, head pounding, thirsty but too nauseous to drink. My stomach rumbled and ached. Ah what romantic nights for me! This was my life at college, night after night. While others went out to socialize I spent my time binging and preparing for an evening with the toilet, all for the purpose of numbing my shame and punishing my body. It came to a point where I could not go on any longer. I had no friends. I was all alone. I cried all of the time. Finally I called my parents and decided to transfer to a school near my treatment center and therapeutic support system. Still I was able to explore every possible issue tied to the bulimia accept for the rape.

Some how I floated through college and found myself two semesters from graduation hiding under my desk in my dorm room, trembling because it was dark outside. I knew I could not go any farther in life until I dealt with my haunting past. I told my roommate what was going on inside of me. She stroked my hair and sang to me while tears streamed down my face. A few weeks later I packed up my Volkswagen and drove home. I got a part time job, lived with my parents and waited. I was not certain what I was waiting for. Then it happened. An episode of 'Felicity' aired, featuring a date rape and a phone number to call for help. I began to sob. My heart ached like never before and I picked up the phone. The next week began an intense eight months of therapy. All I did was work at the Limited, go to therapy and lay curled up on my bedroom floor crying, wailing in agony from all the pain I felt. I felt such sensations of shame, filth, deep pain that literally hurt my heart. I could not escape the pain. Some nights I would fall asleep, uncertain of how I would survive the night with the pain I felt inside. Then the morning would come with new mercies and I could breath a sigh of relief.

The day came when I noticed that I could feel the pain in the safety of my bedroom, in the safety of who I was, KNOWING God was comforting me – and I could live through it then move on to the next part of my day. Some nights I would light a candle, wrap myself in a blanket and lay in a corner of my room because that is where I felt safe. Tears would stream down my face onto the carpet, blood vessels broken around my eyes. Out, out, out tumbled the pain. Then came the point when I was ready to put on paper what he did to me. Each way he violated my body and soul. It took hours to complete because I kept erasing what I had written for fear someone would see. I was even afraid to see it on paper! But I did it! I actually put it out there on paper and then I lit it with a match and watched it burn. I breathed a sigh of relief, flushed it down the toilet and smiled in the mirror. I felt so free because I flushed what he did to me instead of flushing vomit trying to *hide* what he did. It has not been an easy road by any stretch of the imagination, but I am a new person. I am a healed and free person. I am a whole person.

Since that time I finished school and actually moved back to where it all occurred! I have an amazing supportive husband and a beautiful life. I am very much aware each morning when I wake up free and smiling! I ran into my rapist once. Just before I got married I was out reading a magazine and he actually sat down next to me. He did not recognize me. My head was down and I was wearing a ball cap. As soon as I heard his voice and smelled his disgusting cologne I knew it was him. My heart raced. What could I do? Do I leave? Do I wait for him to recognize me? Then my heart rate began to slow down, my breathing was steady. I was free. He would no longer intimidate me. I turned to him and said 'Hello Joe.' He looked at me and said 'Oh my God,' and I got up and walked out of the store.

It took a few moments, but suddenly I realized something — I was smiling!

Dream

Day to day living wondering what it is all about
Wishing I would wake up and find this all a dream.
Haunting words always running through my mind – what could have been, what should have been.
I find you invade my dreams
And there I was as if almost asleep holding a babe in my arms and galloping wildly through the snow
Grasping for life and semi-concious all at once
Leaning into the soft white fur and the safety of knowing I am with you.
Then I am at your doorstep and the babe is safe.
Warmth floods out of your doorway but I do not enter
I sink to my knees and lean against the door frame, weary and almost asleep.
Then I am with you.
I have found the one whose voice I hear again and again.
I wonder why you did not find me.
I wonder still how I ever found you again – I am at rest.
Somehow I am at rest and I feel safe but lifeless as I watch my beloved walk out the door.
Oh echoing wind and moonlite and sun – the evening chases after you – so many colors on the run.
At last my mind stops my heart is at rest.
I draw a breath
It warms my lungs and for a moment peace has found me.
Halfway between where I am and what could have been
So much stolen
Robbed of my dreams
What happens next
Where do I turn
How far does your mercy extend
Unmerited grace will you come my way on the eve of near destruction
Will I bare the mark of your sin forever?

I should have known better some would say
Faith, Hope and Love all of these I had
My redemption is sure to come with the sunrise.

-Rose-

My Friend

I lay silently beside you
I watch and listen
What haunts your dreams
Who calls after you
Why do you listen?
You shake and tremble
You groan even yell
You wrestle with silent memories too dark to tell.
Yet He has called you
He has saved you
He is forever by your side.
Shatter the bottle that holds your tears
Unlock the closet that hides the lies
You are free – walk in your freedom
You are whole not torn apart
For His love mends even the most destroyed heart.
Your spirit longs to sing
You sing healing notes to heaven
He has captured them all now let them rain down on men.
Open heart aching eagerly waiting
Sitting silent staring at a nameless giant
You have a name given to you from above
Arise precious child to face your fears with songs of endless love.
Cast off the dark shadows
Warm your face in the sun
The former things can not hurt you...a new day has begun.

-Rose-

88

MINUTES TO MIDNIGHT
By Steve Augustine

For some those words might be a title to a new CD, they might be a time that comes every night that you just happen to catch while looking at the clock. To me that's what I remember doing counting the minutes to midnight. Up until very recently I've been on an emotional roller coaster with my past. Now I have decided to take control of the ride pull the breaks, step off and watch it from the platform. It will never be erased from my memory but I will no longer let it control my life. This is my story. When I was 12 years old days before my 13th birthday I was already half way through the first session of a two session sleep away summer camp. It was my first time really on my own away from known friends and family. My parents had let me "spread my wings" finally and I was hoping to take full advantage and enjoy the summer. I was and still am a quiet kind of guy. I'm shy till I get to you know, very laid back and when I was younger kept to my self when around strangers. Which apparently made me a target by one of the camp counselors. Everyone had mixed emotions about him. He was weird and creepy at times. We would always catch him watching us when we showered and changed. Every night after 10pm when lights were out only one counselor stayed in the cabin to watch the kids. The others were allowed to leave and enjoy the evening. On one particular evening this counselor woke me from a sound sleep. He shined a flashlight on me and said "be quiet come on down here I want to show you something." I looked at my watch and it was about 10 minutes to midnight. Everyone else was asleep and he brought me to the middle of the room on the floor. He asked me If I would get undressed for him. I told him no and I attempted to go back to my bunk. He then grabbed me by the shoulder and took a small pocket knife and placed it near my throat. He said to me If I didn't do what I was told he would kill me. My body froze but my mind seemed partially active and let my body become limp to his commands. Even though my body was frozen my mind was still forced to be active. As he was forcing me to do things so perverse and so disgusting I tried desperately to keep my mind unfocused on the obvious. I started counting from one to sixty in my head knowing after doing it ten times it would be midnight. I thought maybe there would be a fairy tale ending so to speak and that when midnight came it would all be over. To this day I don't remember how far I had counted. Eventually the main bunk house door opened and other counselors started making there way in, making him jump up in a panic. I was told later if I had ever mentioned the events he would kill me. The next day when everyone was away I found the knife and wrote a letter to the director of the camp and handed it to him as soon as I saw him, and he said that he would take care of it. Later that day I was told by the director that the police had come and taken him to jail and not to worry any more, and to "just keep this between us OK?"

Well, I did for five years which seemed like 500. My best friend then finally convinced me to finally speak up to my parents. Those were some of the worst years of my life now looking back. The "real me" had shriveled up and disappeared and out came this angry at the world person that I didn't know. Then came the lawsuit which in itself was hell. Between having to repeat the story in the gravest of detail over and over to attorneys who thought I was lying in depositions, to attorney appointed psychologists. The defendants side said "You know, I think your gay. Your afraid of telling your parents, so you came up with this story." Our psychologist was only "helping" me in the sense of "OK your not expressing enough depression, you need to have more bad dreams if you want anyone to believe you." All that and more went on for a couple of years then the last chance to stop it from going to court came. It was time for the last mediation before court. I'll never forget my feelings, I couldn't take it all anymore it was destroying me and my family. I told my mom before she left that if there wasn't a settlement of any kind that I would not be home when she got back. When it was all said and done they walked out with just enough to cover attorney costs. It was a joke, but it was finally over.

Now here I am today. I'm 25 years old. Even though I feel older and it seems like I wasn't able to be young for that long it is an experience that has definitely changed my life. For the longest time the Internet was nothing more then prodigy and message boards so I never knew about places like RAINN. I let it control my life, it effected my life in a lot of ways. It hurt a lot of relationships I was in because I didn't know how to deal with it. Since getting involved with RAINN my life has done a total

360 and I'm back to the person I always knew I was. Some have asked me believe it or not would you go back and change the "afterwards?" No, simply because it has given me the chance to be in this position and help someone. I don't want my story to discourage any guy or any girl for that matter from trying to seek justice. I want you to see that no matter who you are you are strong, you can get through anything, and don't let anyone or anything get in your way of whatever legal victory you see fit. Man, Woman, Old, Young, your in control, there is help.

Older Wiser and No Longer Hurting
By Rev. Lady 'Spirit Moon' Cerelli

Ellipses and quotes at the beginning and the end of paragraphs indicate excerpts taken from my book, "My Journey to Peace with PTSD" by Lady Cerelli. Some contents have been taken out for a condensed version; and added paragraphs in between the quotes are for clarity.

When I was seven my father had sat me on his lap and offered me fifty cents to do something for him. I had no idea of what it would be, but I trusted him. He carried me to his and Mom's bedroom. Drunk and stumbling, he tossed me on the bed and undressed me. He tried to penetrate me. But when I screamed out and he saw the blood between my legs, he forced me to give him oral sex.

"…A few weeks later Daddy startled me out of a deep sleep in the early morning hours. Frightened, I became instantly awake when I smelled the alcohol on his breath as he again carried me out to the kitchen and put me on his lap. This time when he asked me if I wanted to earn fifty cents, I mutely stuck out my hand. Remembering not getting the money the last time, I felt brave at having conquered him when he put two quarters in my palm. I wasn't going to chance losing any money again and put out the other hand as I stared at him with tight lips. Blushing, he hesitated only for a moment before putting two more quarters in my other palm. Hatefully, he stated, "I'll hurt your brother if you cry like a baby."

Like a good little girl, I did what I was told. I wondered why Daddy didn't wait for Mom and take her to bed. More often than not, I had the childhood fancy that a monster took over Daddy's body at those times. I began to notice other things about him and wondered what I had done for him to have changed so drastically. Sometimes I doubted these things happened in other families. A week or two later we were in his bed for the third time. There were just threats this time, no "I love you" and no money. I tried my best to keep from breathing so I wouldn't smell his breath. His body smelled bad, too, and he was impatient. Then Mom walked into the room. For an eternal moment the thunderbolt silence stopped my heart and Daddy's breathing while Mom froze in her tracks. In a flash and in one stride, she stepped over to the bed. With a hand of steel she hauled up my hefty body by one arm, and snarled, "Get your ass into your own bed." I was shocked. Mom had never treated me roughly like this before. I was shocked further by again not knowing what I had done. Having raced back to my own bed, I lay there and listened to them arguing, using words I had never heard before. Then silence descended – no noise of any kind. My chest thumped harder and I held my breath. I didn't know what to expect as fear, like acid, filled my throat. In the hard silence, I heard a dresser drawer yanked open and slammed shut with such a loud force that my body jerked in bed. My curiosity got the better of me. I quietly slid out of bed, trying not to disturb my sister. At my bedroom doorway, I quietly dropped to my hands and knees, slowly twisted my upper torso, and peered around the partition into my parents' bedroom. I was certain they could hear my heart because it was beating so loudly. The light from the alley shining through the dirty window silhouetted Mom pointing a handgun at Daddy as she said in a hard whisper, "Touch her again, I'll kill you." The next day Mom would neither talk to me, nor look at me. My heart ached worse than my arm as I teetered on the verge of tears for most of the day. I didn't understand what made her angry with me. The morning hours dragged by and it wasn't until late afternoon that I finally found the courage to speak. I patted Mom's arm to get her attention. "Mom, Daddy pees in my mouth when he takes me to bed with him." I wanted her to be as mad at him as she was with me. She sat staring straight ahead as her lips tightened into a straight line. She was so quiet, I wondered if she had heard me. I touched her arm again, "Mom..." Shrugging my hand away and responding in a tight, angry voice, she said "He didn't pee in your mouth. You just dreamed it." Dumbfounded? Yes. Betrayed? Definitely. How could I have dreamed that? What was wrong with her? The look on her face as she stared straight ahead told me she wasn't going to say anything else. So I crept back to the room I shared with five other sisters and one brother and stayed in bed, alone, until dinner time. I remained confused for a long time after that. Mom and I stopped talking altogether. My world had forever changed yet again on the night Mom walked into their bedroom and found me and Daddy in bed. It wasn't my doing and there was no one I could turn to..." Granny was tiny in build but her character was strong. Looking at her, you knew she was a mountain woman. She wore wire-rimmed glasses, a ready smile, and had a whispering laugh. She was everyone's favorite person. She stayed with us for a couple days twice a year when she came north. Granny was the only one who hugged me at that time of my life; and I followed her around like a starved kitten. "…We were in the basement talking quietly while doing the laundry. It had been four years since Daddy had hurt me and the `nightmare' stayed with me. I still dreamed of seeing Mom with the gun and remembered what she had said. When the washer and the two tubs had drained and Granny and I were wiping them out, it occurred to me to ask her the question burning in my mind those four long, troubling years. "Granny, can I ask you something?" I held my breath. "Yes, child." She looked at me with a soft smile curving her mouth. She always smelled of the rich, pleasant mixture of snuff and peppermint. I related to her what had happened that night when Mom had found me with Daddy. Lowering her eyes, it was a few moments before she raised her head. "Have you talked with your mother about this?" Silence stilled my heart for half a beat before resonating off the walls and around the room, surrounding us. "Yes. But she tells me it was a nightmare." Then I forced out, "And I know it wasn't, Granny," and I started crying. Mom's rejection was still an open wound in my heart. It also hurt because she hadn't trusted me with the truth. The bare light bulb over our heads cast a dingy yellow glow. A shaft of sunlight coming in through the small, square basement window highlighted dancing dust motes in the thick air, full of the damp, earthy odors of the basement. The smell of bleach still clung as the sound of water dripping into the floor drain intensified in the silence. My heart pulsed in my throat, drying it out. I would dissolve in that pool of water in which I stood if Granny, too, told me that it was a nightmare. I could not bear it if she, too, had turned on me. She looked at me, and I saw tears well up in her eyes and fall on her cheeks as she whispered, "Child, I cannot speak to you of this." She then gave me a hug that felt different from any I had ever received from her before. Turning around, she walked through the other room and up the stairs, her soft footsteps echoing in the thick silence. Each drop dripping into the drain sounded like a small explosion to my ears. As my heart beat fell into rhythm with each drop, my trust in my family drained away. With each beat of my heart, my trust in love flowed out into the city sewer. In those moments, loud with silence, I realized three things: I wasn't crazy after all because I now knew I hadn't dreamed the nightmare; I would never lie to another no matter how much the truth might hurt; and since I wasn't able to rely on anyone, I would always stand alone..." All during my growing up years, I knew my insecurities and ineptness had stemmed from my stepfather raping me, and seeing and tasting my own blood. With continued emotional neglect and abuses, behavior disorders set in and my low self-esteem set me up to be a prime target for the military rape when I was 19. I had joined the Navy after high school and finished IBM school. I suspected my pregnancy before transferring to another base. Soon after the transfer I was on a date where I was given a drink laced with drugs and was raped while unconscious and lost the baby. I suppressed the memory of that rape until forty years later when it came back as a flashback. I spent a week in a VA Hospital followed by several months of therapy. It was during an interview with a psychiatrist that I became aware of how the mind can actually kill. "...The female psychologist was nice and I liked her at first, but her questions dredged up memories like a backhoe digging up garbage, one shovelful at a time. I became agitated, ready to cuss her out. "What do you mean, 'How did I feel about the rape?' I wanted to castrate the bastard." Stupid bitch! She turned her chair toward me and asked, "Have you had any miscarriages? " Surprised by her question, I responded, "Yes, all of them." "How many was that?" "Six." She turned back to her computer and started typing. I sat there, dumbfounded, in the quiet room. The silence soon rang with each click of the keyboard. Each tap clicked louder and louder until each click tapped my skin like a tiny electric shock. What do the deaths of six babies have to do with anything? Why is that important? The silence stretched on as my chest squeezed my breath, preventing it from leaving my body except in a slow, narrow stream. My thought processes stopped after slogging through a quagmire. Then a dark, forbidden, lone thought crept in like a deadly shadow in front of my mental screen, forcing me to look at it. I tried to push it away, but I was held immobile in the chair. Please, God. Have I not been punished enough? After that, the psychologist didn't ask too much about the flashback, but asked about my childhood and my teenage years. I managed to answer her questions, but my throat burned with bile drawn up from my stomach. The nausea wouldn't pass and stayed with me during the drive home. I was pregnant when I transferred to the new base. The blood in my flashback wasn't all from an internal injury. The clinical psychologist had told me there were men out there with very large penises. Bill had forced my miscarriage. I knew psychological pregnancies existed. Can there be such a thing as psychological miscarriages? My brain reached out and touched that dark, forbidding shadow, dragging it into the light. I killed my babies. When I lost my last baby during the sixth month, I was told it was due to too many male hormones transferring from the adrenal gland to the placenta. Autopsy on the first baby, also six months in the womb, indicated the same thing. The four babies in between were aborted between three and four months into the pregnancy. There's no way of knowing for sure, but I'm certain that every time I became pregnant, my adrenal glands, through my own psyche, secreted excess hormones until a hormone imbalance eventually aborted the baby. I also suspect the subconscious memory of the original rape that aborted my baby was what psychologically triggered my adrenal glands. This interview was powerful to me for it was absolute proof that the mind can kill. My nightmares were bad, but, so help me, my waking hours weren't much better. There were times, if I stood still long enough, I'd hear strange noises: the clinking of filled drinking glasses; soft voices, laughing; deep voices of men in a huddle. The voices didn't talk directly to me, but I began to wonder if I was schizophrenic. I sat at my computer for long hours playing Free Cell game or Solitaire, or searching the Internet, anything to quiet and divert my thoughts. Tears, waiting just behind my eyelids for a glance or a word of any kind came too easily, too many, and too spontaneously. Sketchy, fragmented memories affected my short-term memory, because I used so much mental energy trying to piece them together. There were times I couldn't remember what I had been told five minutes before and, feeling foolish, wouldn't ask the person to repeat what was said. The memory fragments either took up a large space in my brain, or created a great void. When I said what I thought was in my mind, the information came out in fragments, or not precisely the way I meant it to come out. Crowds became a real problem. If I walked into a room I'd immediately search for all the exits, should I get trapped for some reason. I tolerated loud noises for a while, but eventually I'd have to leave the room when the noise became a loud buzz or a drone in my head, setting my nerves on edge and sometimes giving me a headache. I had always jumped at sudden noises. Now, tiny, sometimes imagined, noises made me jerk, always edgy. And sensitive! I was beyond it, sometimes even paranoid. What did they mean by that? What do they want from me? What do they want me to do? What do they want in return? My brothers had teased me about being gullible when, in fact, I had simply trusted everyone. I'd always searched for that someone in whom I could place my confidence. Trust was now a real issue. I even began questioning my trust in Jim. Could I believe everything he told me? I was afraid to go to bed. Though my antidepressant medication helped me to sleep, it didn't assuage my fear of dreams. I moved around in the daylight, but was afraid that anything I did or said would bring on another flashback. I kept away from people as much as I could. The sessions with Jan helped me to keep my sanity while trying to establish what I felt was a new life. She was my lifeline through what I felt was a surreal life. The antidepressant medication kept my spirits up, but it didn't stop my fears: fear of another flashback, new or old; fear of people; and fear of noises. Fears were alien to me; I had not been afraid of anything prior to the original flashback. I struggled daily with my dilemma of keeping something foreboding pushed to the back of my mind, or allowing it to come forth. I lost interest in my fiber art and my studio collected cob webs. I didn't know what I wanted to do, or even if I wanted to do something. I lost interest in gardening; I used to enjoy playing in the dirt and getting dirty. Spiders in the greenhouse spun their webs, free from intrusion. Looking through the greenhouse window, I often wondered if my memories were pretending they were spiders, intricately weaving their webs with holes and strings going to nowhere, but somehow connecting. Usually, I just sat in my rocker and read, or rather, tried to read; I often just stared off into space. Reading the PTSD description, I immediately latched onto the word "helplessness." This word resonated with each and every trauma I remembered. Helplessness, in my experience, is not an emotion, but a state of mind, a state of "no control." You have no tools with which to deal with your trauma. No words to express your anger. For a few moments nothing registers. Nothing! The shock is so great there's usually no thought that can penetrate into the psyche when the brain is under such stress. In moments of horrific shock, my psyche imprinted upon my brain, not only the visuals of the scenes, but one or more of my five senses. After this moment of helplessness that lasts for a heartbeat, there's an instinctive reaction to freeze, flee, or flight. My first reaction was to freeze. I often wondered if, in my youth, I had been given the tools to deal with abuse or traumas, if I would have learned to fight or flee, rather than freeze. I also wondered if low self-esteem caused me to freeze, thinking I didn't deserve any better and, therefore, zoning out during the abuse. In my adult life, it took only an imprinted sense or a word to send me back to the past to virtually relive the trauma. I recall reading somewhere that prey, running from its hunter, may run for a while then just stop, drop to the ground, and wait for its fate—an internal sense telling it there is no escape. If time passes, and by some miracle, the prey is still alive, it will stand up, do a heavy shiver dance to shake off the trauma, then walk away, seemingly none the worse for wear. Even though we are animal based, humans cannot always shake off life-threatening traumas. I've learned with and through my clients and by my own experiences that the only way we can prevent it from living deep within us is to share it. With no one to share the trauma, and no internal understanding or coping tools gained from a similar experience, I had devised ways of internalizing the trauma as best I could. Unfortunately, "the best I could" wasn't enough and further deepened the pain. Once I had experienced that state of total helplessness, the elements of fear and ineptness silently programmed themselves into my psyche. At the same time, I subconsciously created and put into place the first ember or spark of anger. Psychologically, I used the mortar of tears and spent emotions to cement into place the first invisible stone wall I thought would protect me, and I spent my life building on it. Each instance of a minor or major trauma would resonate with this wall when I remembered or re-experienced a small part of the visual trauma, or if one of my senses was again used to bring on a memory or create a new memory. With each fear or incident of ineptness experienced after the first trauma, I added a coal of anger to those already smoldering. Had the first trauma (ember) been put out by my somehow dealing with it right after the event, or within a short time, the ember would have died. As it was, it smoldered long enough to spark a fire. This fire of anger intensified with the addition of other embers. This fire eventually turned into rage. This rage became so viable it took on its own entity; it was the silent entity that I felt behind me all the time. This was the it that stood waiting expectantly, like a stalking, salivating, wild beast. My psyche was aware of it but couldn't comprehend what it was or why the invisible thing felt so real. Fearing it had taught me to stay in front of it, to keep it behind me. This fear, stemming from the raging fire of anger within me, was the basis for my road rage, spiking anger, and sudden shifts of emotions so dramatic that others wondered if I had a split personality when I suddenly turned on them. Anger, for the most part, was the only emotion I felt and it pushed down all others, numbing me. Anger drove me, though it didn't present itself like anger. It made me super efficient so that it took more than one person to replace me whenever I left a job My mind never shut down, never stopped. It often looked for different ways to do a thing because the old way was no longer interesting. I quickly became bored with jobs and felt the need to get another one, as different and as challenging as possible. Counseling others taught me that anger can create another personality within you, and if allowed to grow, will become its own entity. This personality can take on and make strong a certain trait. This trait, growing stronger, will perform certain tasks; i.e., if you're nervous about taking tests or talking back to another, your stronger personality trait will take over these tasks. If the new personality becomes strong enough, it will take over and suppress you. You may not be able to remember what the stronger personality has said or done. This entity called anger comforted me; justified my screw-ups; justified my hurting others; and was true to me and wouldn't turn on me. Sometimes, it forced me to face up to another, giving me a false sense of courage, strength or intellect; it turned me into a bully. The entity had become such a good friend I was abhorred at the idea of forcing it to leave. Even though my psyche had created this entity within me, I wasn't aware of its powers until someone or something showed me the behaviors this demon created—each behavior as unique as I was because of my life experiences. Even then, my friend, anger, would convince me the person pointing out the behaviors was wrong. My anger was a fire so alive that its excitement wasn't comparable to anything else. I constantly searched for external excitement to equal the exciting fiery anger within me. As all things in the universe, there must be a balance, my psyche sought external means of equalizing the internal self. The term is "self-medicating," and these actions created behavior disorders, sometimes compulsive, like drug/alcohol abuses; surrounding myself with "stuff" because I didn't feel loved; excess food intake; spending money; sex for the euphoric sensation during climax; racing anything on wheels; any perilous act that put me at risk for that ultimate thrill, my need to defy. I recalled what an adult advocate said one time about an abused woman. The woman was asked why she left a relationship with a man who loved her, gave her a good home, and supported her and her children. She responded, "It was too boring." The key word being boring. She was unaware of the fire within her because the fire burns very quietly, its intensity very cold. I now understand that the woman was only aware of the external need to be excited. Hence, she provoked a fight that brought on abuse followed by the honeymoon period; the stage where the abuser asks for forgiveness and acts the lover. The excitement of the abuse, the sex that follows, sometimes followed by alcohol or something to smoke as a sense of celebration, is what the woman sought. For a while, she was satisfied... but only for a while. The fire needs the continual external fuel. When the same adult advocate asked an abuser what it was about a woman that told him he could abuse her, he replied that he could watch a woman walk across the street and know if he could abuse her. He named four traits: 1. Rounded or sloped shoulders—the fire is a great burden. This trait is the most prevalent of all the body languages for those with low self-esteem. 2. They will walk with small steps, will not step out. 3. There is very little eye contact—the lack of courage to "face" another. This one was different for me. I held eye contact. But others don't want someone to think they are being confronted and they don't want to invite a confrontation. 4. They continually apologize by starting their sentences with "I'm sorry...." This can also be seen in body language. I've discovered through my own body language, and that of some of my clients, behavior patterns stemming from a state of helplessness, in both men and women. From the first experience of having no control, control became an obsession—a lot of times overpowering anything else. My body language and the psychological reasons involved with my anger mirrored others I have witnessed in my various careers, and in those I have counseled. 1. Rapid and/or constant speech—fear of hearing the embers crackle or a spark would burn me if I stopped; the need to psychologically keep it a good distance in front of it, so I ran with my speech. 2. The need to dominate the conversation or be the center of attention—I felt like I was floundering and didn't want to drown, get lost, or be ignored. 3. My hands flew, usually in the faces of others, as I spoke. Though I enjoyed the attention, low self-esteem deemed me unworthy, so I felt the need to push people away. 4. Arms folded across the chest—the protective stance. This trait is prevalent with everyone if they are discussing something sensitive to themselves, or if they fear being hurt. It is a move to protect the heart. This was also my way of saying, "No matter what you say…." Much like standing in defiance with my hands on my hips. When my hair was long, I would move my head to move it out of the way or out of my face. This is similar to a mental karate stance. Someone preparing themselves for defense. 5. I became efficient, worked overtime hours to do what I thought others could not or would not do to my satisfaction. I was an overachiever, doing the work of two or more people. Work was also a distraction. I never wanted accolades, but they would sometimes spur me on. 6. I was so driven, I strongly lead the office or group or created a cause to which I could give my energy, usually my all. This gave me my purpose in life. 7. All of my careers were in a field helping others. I couldn't do anything for myself, so I did for others. I guess I was also looking for answers, especially if I was aware of something amiss in my own character. I was so focused and driven that I sometimes wore blinders to everything and everyone in my immediate surroundings. This focused drive masked or shut down other emotions, enabling me to live on a day-to-day basis. "Living a life of quiet desperation" is an apt description. I'd bounce from job to snack, to phone, to snack, then maybe to just a small glass of wine, or to outrageous sex, then the next day, perhaps, to another job. When my anger spiked, I might say or do something to hurt another. Upon hearing what I had just said or seeing what I had just done, I'd become contrite and apologize profusely and try to make up for it. Not understanding what was going on with my mood swings and acid tongue, I never kept friends. Eventually it was better to be left alone than to go through the hassle of forming a relationship only to shatter it. If folks were uncomfortable with me—oh well. My internal fire became a friend so familiar that it inspired me to build a stronger wall. This inspiration became so strong, so invasive, the distraction of it caused me to mishear or miss entirely what was said or not see what was done. I fed on it. Indeed, it became my food, my shield, the anger became the very reason I got out of bed in the morning. It made me feel alive. It kept me alive. The positive side to this internal rage was its ability thrust me into creativity. I'd go into my studio and create something. In my fifties, I was in the gym working out and rediscovered what moving the body does for the brain. I even trained for the senior competitions in racket ball. I realized that I wasn't working for training purposes, but, rather, to get out excess anger. I recognized my anger, but didn't understand from where it came or why it was there. I now understand how a trauma isolated within us gains strength. Once it is shared, it no longer has a foundation on which to build. When we face the original hurt, we actually crack the foundation to which all other hurts, pains, and traumas have attached their tentacles, each turning into a stone placed on the foundation. Every time we share a connecting dot to that trauma, we lose a stone in the wall, as the trauma loses its control over our lives..." Going over this submission for the book, I'm pleased to say that I'm no longer the individual I was last fall when the book was published. It did take its toll on me physically, though. Right now I'm doing things for myself as well as seeing an acupuncture to put my body back on line, as it were. I plan to set aside time for myself each and every day for the rest of my life, because I'm worth it. I'm even looking forward to the workshops we will start this summer. I had decided to not to put out a newsletter, but the feedback from those reading my book will have me do otherwise. We plan to put out the first newsletter this summer. Our non-profit organization, with the website Peace with PTSD.org, is geared towards creating a safe place on the web and in the newsletter for victims to share their traumas and to give others notice that they are not alone. We also plan to have professionals put in their thoughts as well. Our funds are generated in house with the sale of the book, newsletter, and workshops, which should also start up this summer. Our profits go to our small community for the children and elderly; and the other half of the profits go to women and children coming out of the shelters and are seeking their own place. We would like to eventually give out scholarships to the victims. Everyday I pray for women all over the world. I know of very few people in my lifetime who have not been affected by abuse of one form or another, even if they just know someone who has been traumatized. I embrace every woman who survives and do what I can to help her. In my heart I praise every woman who has the courage to stand up and say, "Hell no, you don't have permission to hurt me. I am Woman." Below is the Survivor's Psalm, written by Frank Ochberg, MD, author and founder of the Gifts From Within website. Dr. Ochberg is a

PTSD survivor. I have permission to use it. A copy of this psalm is still pasted on shelf door of my desk. Know you are loved. Survivor Psalm I have been victimized. I was in a fight that was not a fair fight. I did not ask for the fight. I lost. There is no shame in losing such fights. I have reached the stage of survivor and am no longer a slave of victim status. I look back with sadness rather than hate. I look forward with hope rather than despair. I may never forget, but I need not constantly remember. I was a victim. I am a survivor.

My Dear Friend

Oh pretty lady with eyes so bright, so clear, blue and piercing
What bitter thing has caused such fright that awakens you from sleeping?
Your tears seem endless
Memories invade your dreams
The horror of the past grips you while life roles on like ocean waves.
So long I have known you
You have grown older and your heart has softened like a child.
When will you ease your pain and speak?
Release the truth.
Declare it loud and clear
You need not suffer alone!
In darkened hours amidst endless sorrows there is peace forever more.
Joy come flood her being in time of evening that angst may leave her soul.
Oh waves of mercy sweep over her and still her once again.
Anxious heart convulse no more your rest has come within.
Hours tick on the days rush by swift and mighty comes the end.
His Kingdom come His will shall be done and tears find relief in an instant!

Free At Last

From where does such passionate love come?
My heart cries out with joy
My soul dances to the tune of peace.
I fall asleep and drink in quietness...I Am Not Afraid!
No teardrops of pain
No mourning
No clawing my way to day break.
My mind no longer spins on the same course.
All is at rest within me.
At one with my Maker!
My songs are endless
My tears are of adoration raining down and calling out to the One I could never live with out.
Oh my Maker, my God, the Lover of my soul – You have embraced me forever.
I Am Not Alone!

Third In Line

You come with fearful eyes wide open, wondering.
A child in the body of a man.
Mind wandering some where over the rainbow.
Do you even hear me? Can you understand?
So little you leave with so much to comprehend. Does it dance around in your brain until you can no longer stand it?
I wonder when you will be free or if you will at all. I wonder what you are really like and imagine who you are.
How long will you endure this prison? When will you scream and make the walls fall?
Open your mouth, take a deep breath, let your voice be heard!

I AM

So, here it is my life story. I have been struggling with how to start, what to include, what to leave out. I have to smile a bit on that thought, what to leave out. I wish that I had that option of what I could leave out. Most of my life is blank. As blank as this page that I have stared at for so long, walked away from and come back to again and again.

My life as a child was filled with fear. Not fear of the dark, or fear of receiving a poor grade in school. My fear was more primal. My fear was that every day would be my last. I spent every day struggling to survive and live with the knowledge that at any time I would be killed by a boy who lived in our house. To this day the feeling of his fingers around my throat, or his arm on my throat as he shoved my body against the wall, is felt, everyday. Not a single day goes by that I do not feel his hands on my throat. I can't pull my blankets up around me when I get into bed at night. Even the feel of a light, cotton sheet on or near my neck brings back the fear. I can simply slide the sheet down, away from my throat but the images, terror and unfathomable fear is relived, everyday.

I was raised in middle class areas. We moved a lot though. A new house didn't matter to me though, every time our new house was still filled with abuse, alcoholism and chaos. Yet, to me it was very normal. I have very, very few memories of my childhood. I can not remember what my brother and sisters looked like. I do not recognize myself in childhood pictures. I do not remember a single birthday, mine or anyone else's birthday. I can not remember a single Christmas yet in pictures I can see a wonderfully decorated home filled with beautiful decorations, presents and people. I am told they are my family.

It may seem to be an unusual experience to others but as a teenager I can remember looking through old family photos and not knowing who anyone was or where the photos were taken. I would have to work up the courage to ask my mother to tell me who the people are in the pictures. Imagine being a teenager, going through entire albums of family photos and not recognizing nor remember a single person or event. I can remember one time asking my mother who the kids were around a Christmas tree. She looked at me and laughed. "Why can't you ever remember anything? That is you, right there and your sisters and brothers. You were about 7 years old that Christmas" I was shocked. Shouldn't I be able to recognize my family, our house? Shouldn't I be able to recognize myself? All of my life my family would tease me, still to this day, that I never remember anything about my life as a child, really until I was about 12 years old.

I would learn later in my life, much later, that it is not uncommon for victims of trauma to suffer from memory loss. I selected the word "suffer" intentionally. If you knew me you would be surprised because I would never acknowledge that I have suffered. However, the loss of essentially all childhood memories still brings me pain. Simply because I want to remember my sisters and brother. I want to remember school. I want to remember one birthday, or one holiday. I want to remember one kind word or a soft hug. Yet, the memories I do have are of being yelled at, humiliated, violated, strangled and raped. I have many of these memories and they are powerful in many ways. What strikes me most though is my determination and basic, but, strong, primal need to live. I wanted to stay alive so badly. This is a very strong memory for me.

The raping, torture and strangling was done by a boy who lived in our area. The humiliation, torture and indifference that I was treated with came from others as well as this boy. He was about six years older. I was about four. He abused me, raped me and strangled me for the next seven years. He even brought other boys into my room to watch as he raped me. He raped me with penetration using his body parts or toys. He forced me to perform oral sex. I was a child and my memories reflect just how small I was. I always thought that if could be quiet enough then he would not find me. But this boy truly enjoyed tracking me down. It was a game to him, a very, very sick game. He would suddenly open a door and pull me into a room or just laugh because he scared me so much. I have been told by my family that I was the "perfect" child because I was always so quiet, never caused any trouble and was always obedient. I did not want to die. I was quiet and "perfect" because I desperately wanted to live.

Being raped as a child does change you. That is what everyone says. It does more than that though. It changes the world around you. You learn to search for the exit everywhere you go just so you can escape quickly if you have to. You learn to read people quickly and listen quietly, attentively, to learn more about them then they can learn about you. Studying people becomes second nature. Survival is primary. Although it sounds paranoid it isn't. I do not feel that the world is out to get me despite that fact that childhood environment taught me that and instilled it into my mind. There is a difference between being paranoid and having a distinct will and desire to live. I study places that I go to and people that I am with because as a child I always had to be ready to react. To run. To hide. Or to be quiet while he raped and strangled me so that I could live for another day. Wanting to live and growing up learning, literally, how to survive everyday is not paranoia. It is truly a basic, primal need to live that never leaves you.

I first realized this truth in my late teens and early twenties when more and more memories of the raping and stranglings came back to me. I told my parents. They said that they did not know. I can remember being 21 when I told my parents about the rapes and torture by this boy that lived in our area as a child. My mother cried. They both claimed that they did not know. But then they started to tell me about things that they knew that this boy had done to me and others in the house. My mother told me that she caught him twice throwing me down the stairs. She said once she was able to catch me in mid-air, before I hit the landing at the bottom of the stairs. Then she looked at me and said, "But you were okay because I caught you." I was okay because you caught me? Being thrown into the air and down a flight of stairs was nothing in our house I would soon find out. My parents told me that this boy frequently hit my mother and pulled her to the ground by her hair. This boy also beat my father with a bat. My father lost almost all of his vision in his left eye as a result of this beating. I was shocked and confused. Why would anyone let this boy play in or near our house?. I grew up in a world of secrets and it was designed to stay that way. My parents were always telling us that nothing about our family life is to be told to others. They always wanted people to think we were a perfect, middle class family.

I can offer more detail about the rapes and torture that I endured but to do so is unnecessary at this point. So many have endured the same and I do not want to minimize anyone's experiences but adding more detail and making them feel that what I suffered was greater. It was not greater than anothers person's experience; rape at any degree is torture. We should not be comparing the length of time or the severity of torture, abuse and rape from one child (or adult) to another. It is all brutal and it needs to stop. I simply wanted to let others know that the shame, silence and secrets about these horrific occurrences, are not to be kept any longer. It is time that we stop saying that a child was "molested". We must stand up and tell the truth, it is rape. Penetration or not, sexual abuse is rape. Violent. Brutal. Rape.

Although I can not share any good memories of being a child I can share my life's purpose. I can tell you my life's purpose without hesitation. It is to speak for those who have been silenced. Whether they have been silenced by fear, shame, threats, beatings or even death, I will stand and speak for them. I hear stories in the news of children who are abused, kidnapped, raped, beaten and murdered. They are children. Children. I cringe when I hear their tragedies referred to as a "story". They are not a story; they are life, laughter, fear, kindness, curious, afraid, living beings, not a story. I am determined to speak for those of all ages, but especially for children. Regardless of age, they are someone's child; someone's sister; someone's mother, someone's brother, they are a life that must be acknowledged, cherished and protected.

I will stand and speak with others who have had to endure what I have and maybe even worse. I do not know who I was as a child except that I was afraid, desperate to live and wanting to be quiet to survive. I know now that it is time to speak up, to no longer be quiet and to speak for those who can not. I am willing to fight for them, to protect them and to bring to justice those who abuse, torture and rape others. I was lost for many years as a child, feeling so small and insignificant. Now I realize that I am strong, able to help others and determined to prevent abuse of any kind. I now know just who, I am.

By Samantha Montgomery

Printed in the United States
144215LV00002B/57/P

9 781438 942018